Foodservice Marketing for the '90s

A
RESTAURANTS
&INSTITUTIONS
BOOK

Foodservice Marketing for the '90s

How to Become the #1 Restaurant in Your Neighborhood

Tom Feltenstein

John Wiley & Sons, Inc.
New York / Chichester / Brisbane
Toronto / Singapore

Restaurants & Institutions books—co-sponsored by John Wiley & Sons, Inc., and Restaurants & Institutions magazine—are designed to help foodservice professionals build stronger operations.

In recognition of the importance of preserving what has been written, it is a policy of John Wiley & Sons, Inc. to have books of enduring value published in the United States printed on acid-free paper, and we exert our best efforts to that end.

Library of Congress Cataloging-in-Publication Data

Feltenstein, Tom.
    Foodservice marketing for the '90s: how to become the #1 restaurant in your neighborhood / Tom Feltenstein.
        p. cm.
    Includes bibliographical references and index.
    ISBN 0-471-57553-4
    1. Restaurants, lunch rooms, etc.—Marketing. I. Title.
TX911.3.M3F48   1992
647.95′068′8—dc20   92-5621

Printed in the United States of America

10 9 8 7 6 5 4 3 2 1

To all the hospitality and foodservice marketing professionals who have devoted so much time, creativity, and energy to molding our industry. I especially thank all the innovators, risk takers, and marketing pioneers who have made the industry into the titan it is today, and I salute their successors, whom I believe can use this book to continue the rich tradition they've inherited.

Contents

Foreword

It was, I believe, 1985—maybe 1984—that I first met Tom. As for thousands of other restaurateurs who periodically attend the National Restaurant Association "how-to" seminars, this was to be my lucky day.

Tom was conducting the seminar, and I am sure it had been promoted as "Marketing Your Restaurant Successfully" or some such thing. Anyway, I had started my little company in the mid-seventies, and, as many people did during those "better days," ultimately opened a second, and a third. Things were okay, but clearly there had to be a better way—especially if one was willing to make both a philosophical and financial commitment. So, off I went in search of the proverbial silver bullet(s).

It was an experience! By the close of the second day, my mind was literally racing with thoughts of marketing plans, objectives, strategies, and tactics. I had been "saved." The customer truly was "king." And were we ever guilty of "marshmallow" marketing!

Over the years, Tom and I have become very good friends. He has worked for me as a consultant and advisor for my various companies. I have worked with, and assisted him, with the implementation of a "Neighborhood Marketing Strategy" for one of the most well-known franchising organizations in the country. We have worked together, stressing the importance of a marketing plan and all its collateral parts to numerous restaurateurs, independent operators, and "marketing types."

The pages that follow are the Silver Bullet. There is no one simple, magical solution. Knowledge, perseverance, and the quest for excellence from your staff are prerequisites to success, but do not guarantee it. To become really successful in your battle for market share, you will also need to make a commitment to systematically and continually attack your market and to use all the means at your disposal to analyze what is going on within that market and what is going on within your restaurant(s) before, during, and after implementation of your marketing plan.

It is all here! From A to Z, Tom gives you the benefit of his many years in, and service to, the hospitality industry. This is not a book to be read casually. This is a "how-to" book! So, before you even begin reading

Chapter 1, you need to make a commitment to yourself, and to your organization, that you are going to become the best that you can be and that you are systematically going to develop the requisite attitudes, programs, and procedures that will help you succeed.

Tom has given a great deal to the hospitality industry during his professional career. In this book, he gives it to *you*! Whether you are a single-unit independent, large or small, a regional, multiunit operator, or a chain executive, this book will enable you to compete with the best.

Peter Provost, President
Huckleberrys Restaurants
Chairman/CEO
Horizons Publishing

Preface

Since you have purchased this book, you have already bought into the prime advice of management experts when recession looms: Don't just sit back waiting for better times. This strategy does not work anymore. It is an open invitation to your competition to knock you silly. Tough times are your opportunity to succeed if you follow the right marketing system, and that's what you will find in this no-nonsense blueprint.

My system is guaranteed, provided you are tough-minded enough to learn it, execute it properly, and to trust me as you would an experienced coach who is trying to teach you a new way to pass a football, serve a tennis ball, or swim the crawl. Adapting to my system will probably cause you some discomfort, but stay with it and you will experience the joys of a real business breakthrough—of knocking the competition silly, and succeeding in hospitality and foodservice.

My system is presented in what is basically a workbook format. It starts with the field-tested Restaurant Fitness Test, which will give you a clear idea of where your business stands in relation to its true potential. Then, chapter by chapter, you will be introduced to the rationale of marketing planning, building up to strategies and specific tactics. Each chapter is followed by a summary review of chapter highlights.

Don't read the highlights and skip to the strategies and tactics. That will not provide you with the step-by-step instruction you need. My program is a *system,* an approach that is both disciplined and directed toward positive results. You need to read and study it thoroughly.

I have provided a comprehensive glossary of marketing terms that you will need to know in order to become a complete marketer, to deal with advertising and media people, and ultimately to reach your target audience of present and prospective customers. You will also find eight power-packed action appendixes. These are case studies, authoritative articles, and other valuable information telling you how to succeed in hospitality and foodservice throughout the challenging nineties.

In brief, this book contains almost everything you need to steer your business through the perils of the nineties to enormous promise and payoff. What I cannot give you, what you must bring to the game yourself, is a positive attitude, an everyday, all-day commitment to enjoying work, to accepting the challenge without creating undue stress for yourself or for others. And you must share this attitude with all the people in your organization. It can be done, and you can do it! In this book I give you the tools and techniques, but, like the title of the song "You've Gotta Have Heart!" implies, you can't succeed if you complain about the economy and industry conditions, and sit back and wait for things to improve. You have to take charge of the improvement for yourself, while the competition waits.

I want to thank those people who have made significant, not to say essential, contributions to this book. Special appreciation goes to Gene Grennan, a longtime friend and associate, who worked with me on my first marketing book eight years ago. Over many months, Gene has lived with this material at least as closely as I did, providing the writing talent and structural discipline needed to complete this project. I also thank Eileen Walsh Grennan for her invaluable editorial assistance and comment. Barbara Jean Savard, Senior Vice President of Tom Feltenstein Enterprises, managed the often complex logistics of production admirably.

Tom Feltenstein
Palm Beach, Florida

The Restaurant Fitness Test

The Restaurant Fitness Test is not just an idle exercise. You should complete it before you read this book to give you a proper sense of what you need to accomplish and what you are about to accomplish.

To take the test, please check the answers that best describe your operation and record the score in the space provided. After you've finished, total your scores and compare the result with the scale given at the end of the test to determine your restaurant's fitness level.

If you're in charge of a restaurant chain, you can gear your answers in one of three ways: unit by unit; as if each region is one large restaurant; or as if the entire chain is one large restaurant. Of course, you can combine these methods for what may turn out to be revealing comparisons of various regions or the units within the different regions.

THE RESTAURANT FITNESS TEST

		Response Score	*Your Score*
1.	If you were to review business volume over the past few months, would you describe the trend as:		✓
	a. Increasing consistently without price increases	9	_____
	b. Staying even with price increases	6	_____
	c. Declining volume with price increases	3	_____
	d. Don't know	0	_____

2. **What is happening to your customer count?**

   a. Increasing steadily .... 5 _____

   b. Remaining the same .... 4 _____

   c. Declining steadily over the past 90 days .... 2 _____

   d. Don't know .... 0 ✓

3. **What has been the trend of your individual serving periods?**

   a. Increasing steadily .... 4 _____

   b. Remaining the same .... 3 ✓

   c. Decreasing somewhat .... 2 _____

   d. Don't know .... 0 _____

4. **Which comes closest to describing your advertising/promotion activities?**

   a. Run planned programs throughout the year ...... 7 _____

   b. Run ads/promotions on special occasions .... 3 ✓

   c. No advertising promotions to speak of .... 1 _____

5. **How would you estimate your employee turnover rate?**

   a. 10 percent or less over 12 months .... 6 _____

   b. 25 percent over 12 months .... 4 _____

   c. 50 percent or more over 12 months .... 2 _____

   d. Don't know .... 0 ✓

6. **Could competition influence you to vary your menu?**

   a. Yes .... 5 _____

   b. Maybe .... 4 ✓

   c. No .... 2 _____

7. **When was the last time you reviewed where your customers lived and worked and how you could attract more?**

   a. Six months ago or less .... 8 _____

   b. Between six months and one year ago .... 6 _____

   c. Over a year ago .... 2 ✓

   d. Never .... 0 _____

8. **When was the last time you personally talked to a customer?**

   a. Yesterday .... 3 _____

    b.   Within the past week   2   ✓——

    c.   Over two weeks ago   1   ——

    d.   Never   0   ——

9.   **When was the last time you checked on how satisfied your customers are with your food and service?**

    a.   Yesterday   3   ✓——

    b.   Within the past week   2   ——

    c.   Over two weeks ago   1   ——

    d.   Never   0   ——

10.   **How often do you hold training sessions for your service staff?**

    a.   Quarterly   3   ——

    b.   Semiannually   2   ——

    c.   Annually   1   ✓——

    d.   Less than annually   0   ——

11.   **How many visits per month do you make to competitive restaurants in your trade area?**

    a.   Five   5   ——

    b.   Four   4   ——

    c.   Three   3   ——

    d.   Two   2   ——

    e.   One   1   ——

    f.   Less than one   0   ✓——

12.   **Do you have a training program?**

    a.   Yes   1   ——

    b.   No   0   ✓——

13.   **How many hours a week do you set aside for planning?**

    a.   Over three   3   ——

    b.   Between two and three   2   ——

    c.   Between one and two   1   ✓——

    d.   Less than one   0   ——

14.   **When was the last time you evaluated your menu (other than pricing)?**

    a.   In the past two months   8   ——

    b.   In the past four months   6   ——

c.	Over four months ago	2	✓
d.	Never	0	

15. **When was the last time you checked on the population growth and other demographic changes in your area(s)?**

a.	Within the past year	3	
b.	Within the past two years	2	
c.	More than two years ago	1	✓
d.	Never	0	

TOTAL 31

Now see how your total ranks with the following scale:

65+	You're doing fine. Keep up the good work; but stay alert.
51–65	Not bad. But a little extra effort could mean a big difference.
35–50	You've got problems, and you should really be working on them.
34 or under	Don't wait! You need serious help immediately.

Now that you've finished the test and calculated your ranking, you're ready to read this book. As you do, keep in mind seven key issues in foodservice marketing as they relate to your business:

1) What is the current and projected demand for my format?
2) What is the competitive environment?
3) What are the basic strengths of my format and what improvements are needed?
4) Who is my targeted customer and should this target be changed?
5) How effective are we in executing the format at the unit level?
6) How effective and efficient is our marketing effort?
7) Where should I build new units? (as determined by geographic area and by specific site)

Now, you're ready to take off!

Introduction

WHAT IS NEIGHBORHOOD MARKETING?

What would happen if every customer living more than three miles from your business suddenly vanished? Disappeared into thin air? Chances are, you would hardly notice. That's because 80 percent of your sales come from right *inside* that three-mile radius.

Now: are you directing 80 percent of your marketing efforts towards that critical area? Or even 50 percent?

Don't feel foolish if the answer is no. After all, for years we've been brainwashed by the myth of mass marketing. Bigger is better, we've been told. Everyone is your customer. Tell the world about your product, and they'll beat a path to your door. There's just one problem with that approach. It doesn't work, plain and simple. The heydays of mega-marketing are dwindling. Truthfully, they never really existed for neighborhood-based businesses.

Sure, it was easy to justify that five-county TV media buy with great TRPs. But did you ever see a TRP walk into your business? Of course not. *People* walk in and buy from you. *People* like that working mom, four blocks over. *People* like that ambitious salesman in the office building next door. *These* are the people who make or break your business. You can't get close to them when you're busy shouting over their heads.

That's where neighborhood marketing comes in. It's not the wave of the future. It's here right now. Call it what you want: micro-marketing, local store marketing, shrink thinking. Just remember that both multi-national corporations *and* Ma and Pa's corner store are making it work for them. This is not a fad . . . the battle for the heart, mind, and pocketbook of the consumer will be won on a block-by-block, store-by-store, purchase-by-purchase basis.

The interesting part is that neighborhood marketing is being treated as a new concept, which it most definitely is not. It's arguably the very oldest form of marketing. It's old Mr. Johnson at the general store who *knew* that your great great grandmother came into his store every Wednesday and bought a sack of potatoes, two sacks of flour, a jar of molasses, and some candy for the grandchildren—and so he was sure to have those items on hand when she arrived each week. It's that kind of knowledge of and attention to neighborhood customer needs that makes neighborhood marketing so attractive today.

In more modern times neighborhood marketing has taken on some systems and procedures to guide and direct the process, but the fundamental precepts remain.

Neighborhood marketing is neither complicated nor costly—it is not necessary to have an MBA to put it into practice. It is the hands-on mechanics that can be performed by a limited staff at low cost. It is the *action* that produces sales.

The geographic area which can be covered in ten minutes' travel time (in each direction from your restaurant) represents **your trading area,** and what more and more smart marketers are finding is that *the only place you can effectively compete on equal footing with big-budget, big-clout competition is within your own trading area!* In other words . . . use more brains than bucks.

Neighborhood marketing starts in your restaurant—within your own four walls. It circulates to your property line, and then beyond—into your trading area. In order to penetrate that trading area you must consider your unit as a media in itself—one of the best in your town. It ranks right up there with radio, TV, and print. In the immediate trading area there is no waste. *You* create the circulation, the frequency, the penetration into the neighborhood area where your customers are. *You* carry the national advertising programs (the big artillery) down to the local level. *You* do the street fighting—the hand-to-hand combat that is needed to win the minds and hearts of the customers right there in your neighborhood—in the trenches!

When properly applied, this targeted form of marketing brings virtually everything in your trading area into focus as a potential marketing opportunity. All your area retailers, schools, churches, and community leaders are viewed as promotional allies in building short-term and long-term sales and profits. Using community components as potential sources of business, the restaurateur needs to separate those people who occupy the residences, work in the factories, offices, and stores, attend the schools—the heads of families, men, women, boys, girls—into groupings that may be used as targets to market your restaurant. The continual interaction between the restaurant and all the components of the trading area is the foundation of neighborhood marketing.

The effectiveness of this one-on-one local community involvement cannot be questioned, because, as far as the community is concerned, *you are your restaurant!*

Neighborhood marketing provides you with *practical, workable, and straightforward answers* to the complex problems facing foodservice operations in today's highly competitive environment. Neighborhood marketing is a logical, disciplined, proven process. A powerful, persuasive tool, it can be successfully used to:

- **Attract** new customers
- **Boost** average purchase
- **Increase** visit frequency
- **Reverse** sales declines
- **Improve** customer loyalty
- **Heighten** visibility
- **Deepen** trading area penetration
- **Extend** advertising impact
- **Increase** awareness
- **Motivate** staff

You will find that your employees thrive on the local recognition and become wholeheartedly involved in the marketing activities. And, through concentrated neighborhood marketing efforts you will hit target opportunities consistently and cost-effectively for far greater community awareness and customer response.

No matter how complex, sophisticated, or expensive a marketing program is, it all boils down to gaining new customers, encouraging more visits, and realizing higher transactions. These three objectives can best be achieved in the uncomplicated, inexpensive process called neighborhood marketing.

Effective neighborhood marketing requires work and effort. It's deal making at its very best and in its most fundamental form. It's low-cost or no-cost. It's getting others to market your location. It's getting others to send their customers, their members, their employees to your business because you're doing something for them. It can be so effective—all it takes is doing!

Foodservice Marketing for the '90s

The Marketing Perspective: Don't Leave Home Without It!

I was flying home to Florida one Friday night, a full week of intensive work with a new foodservice client behind me. I looked back on seven 15-hour days, days packed with extracting vital information, studying the competition, reviewing past marketing programs, visiting facilities, trying out products, checking service and quality. The all-out effort had led me to some very clear conclusions about the strategic directions my client should take to turn around an ailing, but once very healthy business.

Sure, new competitors had entered the market. Sure, they'd taken a large chunk of business away from my client. Sure, they'd been able to outmuscle my client with big city ad campaigns. But competition alone didn't sicken my client's business. They infected themselves with a losing attitude—becoming complacent and nonresponsive to the competitive pressures.

Throughout dinner on the plane I thought about the week, about the client, about the plans I had helped structure. After my dinner tray was cleared away, I started to review my notes and minitapes to plan followup activities and implement the decisions I had struggled for hours to reach.

As I worked, I was struck with this thought: A good part of the week had been spent rehashing and reselling some very basic foodservice marketing ideas and concepts. In short, valuable time—the client's and mine—had been wasted.

Why? After all, I had been dealing with foodservice marketing pros with years of experience that easily matched mine. Why had I found myself trying to convince them and their bosses of what we probably would all readily agree were self-evident marketing truths?

The more I thought about the week's proceedings, the more concerned I became. If these seasoned, top-level foodservice professionals were losing sight of the basics, what about the people who reported to them? How could they be expected to perform in a way that would return top profit dollars to their operations?

It wasn't long before I was comparing other recent experiences with clients and potential clients and reflecting that basic marketing strategies, proven through the years to be the key to success in the foodservice game, were being given very short shrift when it came down to making plans for the nineties, a time when crowded personal and family schedules should bode well for the foodservice industry.

Marketing strategies focusing on the obvious, but powerfully compelling, need to generate foodservice business through planning at the market level and consequent execution at the local unit level were not being entirely ignored. More insidiously, they had been paid lip service. Their jargon had been written into marketing plans, but their acceptance and incorporation into the business culture had been increasingly overlooked.

Searching for the reasons behind this can be unrewarding. Perhaps, as new generations of foodservice marketers come to the fore, the proven techniques are regarded as "old hat," the attention to detail looked on as unimportant in relation to the larger view taught at some business schools. It's probably more likely that there is an ironic correlation between the success achieved by the localized—as opposed to nationwide—marketing strategies that have sparked the foodservice industry since its formalization in the fifties by pioneers like Ray Kroc and the fact that there is a tendency to underrate their power today.

Many of today's foodservice marketers seem to be asking if a concept that's been around for so long can still be valid. In a world that changes second by second, where fads in food and foodservice flash in and fade out rapidly, don't we need something different?

No matter what others may believe, marketing plans constructed at the market level are still how profit is made in foodservice. Yes, this idea has been around a long time. But during these past decades, it has matured into a discipline that can be described, incorporated into the marketing plans and cultures of foodservice chains, and effectively communicated to all levels of management.

What is probably more important is that the nineties are characterized by general and restaurant industry-specific marketing conditions that, in combination, practically cry out for the proper application of marketing techniques.

Consider these for a moment. There are two emerging general trends that particularly affect foodservice, presenting the now familiar crisis-opportunity option: disaster for the unwary, triumph for the vigilant. First, there is the expansion of the middle class into a vast, highly diverse group with numerous lifestyles. Then, there is an accompanying shift in America's general demographics, which has produced more seniors in the population, a large number of single adults, a greater proportion of women in the workplace, and a predominance of two-income families.

What does this mean to foodservice? As a health-conscious population lives longer, they will demand more nutritional restaurant menus. Traditional family-style dining at home will give way to eating habits shaped by highly selective, individual lifestyles. Women who work all day will be increasingly unwilling to cook at night. More of second incomes will go into restaurant purchases.

These changes, and their effects, run deep. Just look at the nutrition issue alone. Less than 20 years ago, Americans were largely oblivious to the effect of diet on health and longevity. Now, they demand low-sodium, low-fat, low-cholesterol, low-calorie, and low-sugar items. From fast foods to fine dining, nutritional programs are firmly in place; menus virtually teem with words like "slim," "trim," "light," and "fitness." Not only is health-consciousness here to stay, but its thoroughgoing transformation of the foodservice industry is likely to pick up pace, along with other agents of change.

In the seventies and early eighties it was feasible for many restaurant operators to achieve sales growth merely by opening more and bigger locations. It is more typical today to find that markets are oversaturated, that marginal units are closing almost as quickly as new ones open, that weaker chains are likely to be swallowed up by stronger ones, that merely holding the line in foodservice marketing practically guarantees failure.

The National Restaurant Association believes that the crisis-opportunity syndrome is likely to be with us for some time to come. An NRA Delphi panel study identifies the following among the most likely developments in foodservice as the year 2000 approaches:

- Competition will be more intense than it is today.
- New forms of competition will arise to address the need for convenience.
- Major chains will increase their share of sales and units.
- Much chain growth will come about through mergers and acquisitions.
- Unit expansion will slow.

- Off-premises consumption will capture a greater sales share.
- Gourmet-to-go foods and boutiques will be more numerous.
- Independents will be concentrated in the upscale market, where they will dominate.
- Entrepreneurs will be the main source of new concepts.

The study also confirms that service will become an even more important point of differentiation among competing foodservice providers. Also, not surprisingly, the study projects as a least likely development the probability that the foodservice industry will not look much different than it does today.

What does all this add up to for foodservice executives and marketers? It means that a foodservice executive who does not have marketing sensitivity is probably in the wrong business. In few other industries is marketing as integral a discipline as it is in foodservice, and financial and operations people who do not carry marketing savvy as part of their executive portfolio should carry that portfolio somewhere else. This is true even though marketing has become one of the omnipresent business buzzwords of recent years, and it is very unlikely to lose its stature in general business at any time in the foreseeable future.

But marketing holds a very special place in foodservice. The American Marketing Association defines marketing as "the performance of business activities that direct the flow of goods and services to the consumer or user." This means that marketing begins at some point in time after a product is produced.

But in restaurant or foodservice, the main product—food—is literally produced as it is sold. This means that in foodservice, marketing is all-encompassing, involving planning, production, presentation, delivery, pricing, promotion, distribution, and service—with all of these functions synergized in importance and timing.

In foodservice especially, marketing must be dynamic, not static. It requires constant application, attention, and effort, not periodic review and sporadic emphasis. It constantly raises questions that just as constantly and rapidly demand solutions. It is a way of thinking and acting that helps organizations capitalize on opportunities that will provide optimal profitability. In short, marketing is the key to success in the foodservice game.

Marketing is well worth a reverse-angle look that reveals what it is *not*. Marketing is not a random collection of sales and promotional tools. It is not just advertising, sales promotion, public relations, employee relations, research, new product development, word-of-mouth reputation, positioning, quality control, demographic and geographic information, couponing, or discounting. Marketing is all of the above, with each element orchestrated to be in tune and in time with every other element and directed by a marketing-sensitive management that makes the best use of available resources of all kinds.

The importance of each separate element of a marketing plan for the foodservice enterprise is not to be disparaged. Rather, each component is linked to the others. Like a steel chain, a marketing plan is only as strong as its weakest link. Internal inconsistencies, voids, or cross-purposes will weaken the entire plan and negatively affect the results it is supposed to support. To weld the chain securely, you must develop a marketing perspective. Be warned: It is easy for a foodservice organization to mistakingly believe that it has a true marketing perspective.

Take the client mentioned earlier. They had a marketing department. They had a high-powered, highly paid marketing executive. They talked marketing. But they did not have an overall marketing perspective, let alone the market-level marketing perspective necessary for success in the foodservice industry.

What they had was an *operations* perspective. They worried chiefly about operations issues—cost control, quality maintenance, profit building, recruiting and training, and productivity—and rightly so. What restaurant operation can succeed without paying attention to these areas? Operations should not be discarded or replaced. But a marketing perspective should share at least equally in carrying the management burden.

While much of this book deals with the tools of marketing, these tools are useless, even dangerous, unless you and your organization adopt a marketing perspective. There is no bag of tricks that can be pulled out at random. A marketing perspective helps you align your business to serve the needs of well-defined groups of customers or potential customers. Every aspect of the operation is aimed at the ultimate goal of serving customers.

Before looking at the marketing perspective more closely, you need to be aware of another very important concept: the value of a single customer.

One customer, visiting your operation twice a week, spending $8.00 per visit, is worth $832.00 a year. Even more important, whenever you have a repeat customer, chances are that that individual will also bring in at least one new customer. Your first customer is now worth $16,640 in 10 years. Progressing a step further, if a waiter in a sit-down restaurant handles five tables a night, that translates to 5 × $16,640 every shift the waiter works. Taking a longer-term view, a customer who hosts a six-person business dinner twice a month brings about $47,250 to your business every 10 years. One new customer leads to another, and that really piles up the profits and starts you off toward success. The value of a single customer is an important component of the marketing perspective.

THE MARKETING PERSPECTIVE ILLUSTRATED

For this book to really help you and your organization succeed in foodservice, it is essential that you understand the difference between a marketing perspective and an operating orientation. A couple of hypothetical cases will make this point while providing you with a way to test your own marketing orientation—perhaps even to test how your colleagues might react to some situations that could easily be encountered in any restaurant operation.

Case A

Given a choice, would you rather (choose one):

- Serve 100 customers at a $5.00 check average?
- Serve 75 customers at a $6.66 check average?
- Serve 125 customers at a $4.00 check average?

Foodservice people often say something like "I'd rather sell one chicken for a million dollars, instead of 125,000 chickens to make my million." The marketing perspective says "chicken bones" to that kind of reasoning. Lose the one customer and you're out of business. This is quite an exaggeration, but it does illustrate the point.

What was your choice? The marketing perspective chooses the 125 customers at $4.00 check average. The larger your customer base, the more insulated you are against severe volume dropoff due to poor service, competing attractions, or moves from your area. In addition, you should reach more referrals through a larger base, and there are many ways to build your check average once you've consolidated the base.

Case B

The cost of your most popular menu item has increased. What is the marketing perspective option?

- Raise prices proportionately.
- Cut the portion size, but keep the price stable.
- Find a cheaper product so that you can maintain the price.

The marketer will raise prices rather than cut either portion size or quality. Cutting the portion size conflicts with the basic customer desire for an appetite-satisfying amount of food. Likewise, the marketing-oriented manager would never suggest compromising the quality of the most popular menu item. That would jeopardize what might well be the very reason that many people come to the restaurant.

It goes without saying that the marketer should keep the price as reasonable as possible, and explore the viability of some alternatives such as changing suppliers, buying in larger quantities to reduce costs, or inching up prices on commonly ordered side items. The marketer might raise the price but offer a special price for a multiple order.

THE MARKETING PERSPECTIVE IN PLACE

As important as the marketing perspective is, it need not—and should not—eliminate, diminish, or deemphasize other aspects of the operation. On the contrary, the marketing concept clearly works only if the other management functions and operational divisions are totally integrated into the marketing effort.

Further, no marketing strategy will ever meet its objective unless it is operationally practical, implementable, and acceptable to the entire organization. In essence, the total success of your operation is directly proportional to the degree that you are able to match your combined resources with the needs of your customers.

The greater the concentration of resources, the more effective and profitable the results. As light rays are tightly bound to create a laser with power far in excess of the sum of the original rays, so can you increase the profit power of your organization. Management's ability to program all departments and units to focus on the marketing objective and to employ strategies consistent with that objective will determine the success of the marketing effort.

Sure, you say, that sounds good, but in multiunit foodservice the very nature of the business tends to decentralize management and to encourage a free-wheeling, entrepreneurial style. This is not all bad, and in fact is desirable in a business like foodservice, which relies on dynamism to fuel success. However, the situation demands that you take greater care in establishing clearer, more focused objectives, and in creating a unified effort and commitment by all elements of the organization.

Foodservice marketing is a discipline. You're about to see how to make that discipline work for you, whether you're one unit or 100 units, to make you and your company consistently successful in the foodservice business—as measured by your profitability.

CHAPTER HIGHLIGHTS AND REVIEW

1) Lifestyles are changing but foodservice marketing basics remain the same.

2) Competition in foodservice will become even more intense, so the basics and discipline will become even more important.

3) You need a true marketing perspective, but you can easily fool yourself into thinking you already have one.

4) The marketing perspective must pervade all aspects of a foodservice operation.

5) Never underestimate the value of a single customer.

Chapter Two

Marshmallow Marketing, General Patton, and the Mules

The chief obstacles to adopting a true marketing perspective and fully integrating it into your way of doing business are education and position.

Sounds a bit startling, doesn't it? While schooling and organizational rank may be matters of personal pride, it may well be that they are directly interfering with your chances of leading your organization to greater profits and of achieving even greater success in your own career.

You may have taken college marketing courses, attended the latest in marketing seminars, and otherwise equipped yourself educationally for your career. Because you've demonstrated substantial ability, you have attained a responsible position. But, let's examine some of the side effects of your schooling and your successful move up the corporate ladder.

The marketing courses taught at most major schools tend to take a big-sweep, strategic-focus approach to marketing. This marketing methodology is what drives much of American commercial success, and it's undoubtedly the basis of much of the personal "smarts" that have fueled your own career. This methodology has also generated a whole lexicon of business words and terms, many of which you will encounter in this book.

For instance, take the word "marketing." It has become the business newsbite of the early nineties and shows every sign of living lustily on for the rest of the century. "Marketing" is both an everpresent buzzword and the "open sesame" of business. There has been a good deal of indoctrination taking place, however. In business schools, marketers are taught to think big. Your career up to now has seemingly proven that theory to be fact.

This is all great, so far as it goes—but in foodservice it doesn't go far enough. The big sweep, the familiar word, what's brought you ample rewards in terms of pay, power, and perks, will only guarantee foodservice mediocrity. True success is quite another story.

Do you remember the movie *Patton?* General Patton plans a grand strategy to beat the British forces commanded by Montgomery in a race to Messina. The plans are risky, but possible. When it comes down to executing them, however, there are problems moving armored support to the beachhead. In rapid succession, Patton finds a fording area for tanks, replaces a commander on the spot for slow movement, and shoots two mules that balk at crossing a narrow bridge and back up a relief column for miles. His attention not only to strategy but to the details necessary to succeed made the difference between indifferent success and a triumphant march into Messina just ahead of a fuming Montgomery.

Patton was no marshmallow general. He couldn't afford to be, any more than you can afford to be second in the marketplace because of "marshmallow" marketing.

What is marshmallow marketing? It can be defined by describing some of its dire effects on what seemed to be viable restaurant concepts (the names are changed to protect the marketers):

- Le Pomme de Terre died because an orderly restaurant introduction process was ignored. There was no effective feedback mechanism in place to warn management that the customer base was rejecting the concept as originally presented, and this made it impossible to make changes. Moreover, the normal word-of-mouth reputation building never occurred. Despite mass infusions of advertising dollars, the restaurant received the coup de grace.

- Sam's Swift Seafood Shanty drowned in a flood of pricing rejections because it was positioned above the average fast-food price point. Customers couldn't tell that there were quality ingredients being used that "justified" the price differential. Sam's took the Deep Six while other seafood restaurants in the market flourished.

- The Allpoints Restaurant Company went South in more ways than one with a concept that had been successful in the Northeast. Rather than building a pilot unit and testing their relatively simple concept against southern lifestyles, the company built four units simultaneously, stifling its ability to change and draining its credit resources completely.

- The Pheasant was perceived as a special occasion restaurant. The majority of its customers went there only for birthdays and anniversaries and were not encouraged to return for less festive events. The Pheasant celebrated only two anniversaries of its own although the owners had years of sad memorial observances.

While the above examples are dramatic, marshmallow marketing has other effects that are far more subtle, effects that prevent a restaurant from realizing full profit potential and gaining market dominance. Marshmallow marketing can lead to slow marketing death as well as premature demise.

Marshmallow marketing can appear in a variety of forms. To name just a few, there's the marketer who writes a marketing plan that throws half the sound principles and premises of marketing out the window and breaks the rest. Then, there's the one who writes a fine plan, encloses it in a fancy binder, and lets it languish on the shelf. Of course, there's the worst offender of all: the one who doesn't even bother to write a plan.

THE SEVEN SOFT SPOTS: MARSHMALLOW MARKETING IN THE MAKING

Assuming that you have not chosen the worst way to pursue the foodservice business and that you have a marketing plan in place and in operation, look at the following items to see if any of them sounds disturbingly familiar in terms of your marketing plan:

1) Inadequate market information
2) Overlooking the obvious
3) Unrealistic/undefined goals
4) Incompatible market mix
5) Poor follow-through
6) Ineffective promotion
7) Poor internal communication

Ring any bells? If so, pay attention—they're alarm bells. If even one of these items makes you uneasy, your instincts are warning you that something could be eroding the soundness of your plan. If a quick reading of the list doesn't set off your instinctive early warning system, read the following explanation of these items.

Inadequate Market Information

Market information must be accurate. Plans based on inaccurate information are doomed to fail. Simply put, how can you possibly plan a strategy or tactic if you don't really know your marketplace? The answer is: You can't. You haven't a prayer against competition you don't know thoroughly. You've got to know who your competition is, what they are serving, how they are serving it, and the price they place on their product. You've got to know your clientele—where they come from, where they live and work, how frequently they visit your restaurant, and why.

What is the only way?

Research need not be complicated to produce the kind of information that you need. Perhaps you have an elaborate research mechanism in place. Are you sure it is not too elaborate, too costly, too time-consuming? Is it producing data that are immediately obsolete?

Once you've collected accurate and timely information, do you know how to analyze it, how to update it simply and quickly? Are you positioned to use it properly? Are you astute enough to recognize the changes your research turns up? Most important, are you flexible enough to react to that recognition by making necessary alterations in your way of doing business? Finally, are you self-confident and realistic enough to admit your weaknesses when they are highlighted by your research, using that admission as a prelude to corrective action?

Overlooking the Obvious

Remember the old expression, "missing the forest for the trees?" As important as it is to focus intently on your immediate market area, you have to sharpen your peripheral vision as well. This means that you have to be aware of broad changes in customer attitudes.

When you start analyzing your data, look for signs that may anticipate or confirm any general shift in customer attitudes toward food and dining. Remember that the speed of today's communications only accelerates the effect of such shifts.

Who would have thought, for example, that beef-loving Americans would move so far in a relatively short time from such a long-favored product? Beef people were forced to employ folksy and sincere Jim Garner to extol the traditional virtues of their product. Concern for health and weight control have led people to try, and enjoy, seafood, poultry, and salads. (Not long ago, *The National Provisioner,* for almost a century the principal publication of meat industry executives, extended its coverage to include seafood and poultry in recognition of its reader-ship's growing interest in these foods.)

Consider the American auto industry. Industry insiders refused to believe that Americans would ever forsake their love for large, gas-thirsty cars. Foreign car makers gained a foothold because U.S. com-panies overlooked obvious vulnerability in the petroleum supply and obvious demand for more reliable products.

Unrealistic/Undefined Goals

Marshmallow marketers are typically poor goal setters. Either they don't properly evaluate whether the goals they set are appropriate and achievable for their organizations or, having determined an attainable set of goals, they fail to record them so they can be measured consistently.

Goals should definitely be challenging, but they should always take the resources of the organization into account. Some managers set goals that are below what their organizations need to succeed competitively, so when these goals are reached they are meaningless and self-deceptive. On the other hand, overly ambitious goal setters aim so high that they simply frustrate and discourage the entire organization.

Once proper goals have been set, they must be written down and they must be specific. When goals are clearly written and properly communi-cated, those responsible for reaching them will be able to chart a course toward attainment and to measure their progress. For example, if your waiters/waitresses know that you want to increase check averages by 10 percent, it is easy for them to decide how they can help and to check regularly to see if they are helping. It is also easier for you to point out how they can benefit from helping you achieve your goals. This com-monality of focus creates a sense of belonging and teamwork which, in turn, increases employee satisfaction. People want to succeed in their jobs, and are helped tremendously if they understand what is expected of them.

Among the many goals that may be set by a foodservice organization, specific sales goals are of the highest importance and are the key to marketing success. Sales achievement is naturally quantifiable and easily communicated throughout the organization. No serious foodservice or-ganization should be without clear sales goals.

Incompatible Market Mix

The need for a marketing plan to be developed with elements that are both internally consistent and compatible with external market forces is basic and obvious. Yet, consistency and compatibility are violated with amazing frequency. Marketing ideas that look simply great on paper may fail because they are out of line with the rest of the marketing mix, the organization, and the market at large.

These violations, not surprisingly, are often related to or result directly from soft goal setting. When goals are not made clear to all, an incohesive marketing plan is inevitable.

The list of such violations verges on the endless, not to say the ridiculous. Just for illustration, look at the following examples:

- Promoting a low-end pricing strategy with advertising aimed at upscale customers.
- Attempting to expand the customer base by offering and promoting faster service when outlets are already at full service capacity.
- Developing an extensive children's menu at a restaurant offering expensive French cuisine and white glove service.
- Providing loud entertainment for clientele mostly over 50 years of age.
- Opening a first-quality concept unit with highly trained staff and exceptional food without budgeting for quality advertising.

You can see the variety of pitfalls. Perhaps you can add a few from your own experience. All plans must be at once consistent with the needs of the targeted market, the overriding corporate and marketing goals, and the capabilities and resources of the organization. They must also be entirely consistent with all elements of the marketing mix—product, pricing, distribution, and promotion—matched and working harmoniously.

Poor Follow-Through

It is essential that you monitor the results of your plans. Many inspired marketing plans have foundered and many clearly defined and thought-out goals have been unmet because no one bothered to monitor their progress at regularly scheduled intervals. Proper follow-through allows you to see your current status in relation to your goals, giving you the opportunity to adjust your short-term tactics. It is also the vehicle that allows your employees to see how well they are performing in the marketing effort. In brief, if you're not going to monitor progress, don't bother setting goals.

Ineffective Promotion

You can very easily build ineffectiveness right into your promotion. All you have to do is engage in off-base development. Many restaurant owners and managers overlook the most basic purpose of advertising and promotion: to get people to eat in their establishments. So, they choose advertising and promotional campaigns because *they* personally find them appealing, or because the campaigns project a glorified image that satisfies *their* egos. They're caught off-base because they've forgotten that the campaigns must attract customers and evoke positive customer response.

Lack of continuity can also render a promotional/advertising program *Radio — and consistency* ineffective. Repetitive advertising and promotion strengthen your identity. If you stop, or cut back, you short-change your reputation and erode the confidence your customers have placed in you. Left to their own imagination, these customers will conclude the worst—that your business is failing. Then, they will stay away and help it to really fail.

Even when the economy turns sour, smart companies continue to advertise and promote because they know that customer communications is far too precious to sacrifice capriciously. Remember: Advertising and sales promotion funding is investment, not expenditure!

Weak scheduling presents another way of derailing sound promotion. Without a strict schedule, everything goes down the drain. Imagine a customer presenting a coupon only to be put off by an employee uninformed about the promotion scheduling.

Poor Internal Communication

You can't walk around with marshmallows in your mouth. Keep all of your people informed, all of the time.

You have a wonderful marketing plan that is specifically written and based on current research, a plan with peripheral vision, sharply defined written goals, and a functioning monitoring mechanism—but only the top managers know about it. There is no downward communication, or the communication varies in intensity and clarity with each manager's method of sharing important information. Methods of communication may well be limited by territorial or egotistic concerns.

You must provide written direction, use employee incentives, hold seminars or refresher courses, and conduct meetings that include everyone possible at all locations. Your aim is simple: Communicate for greater profitability.

SHOOT THE MULES

You can see how intertwined all these marshmallow marketing warning signs are, and how dangerous they can be to any business. Do you remember Sambo's, Victoria Station, W. T. Grant's, Packard automobiles, and Waldorf Cafeterias? All top names, all gone into oblivion.

What happened to them? Basically, they failed to keep pace with the changing market environment because they conducted marshmallow marketing. They thought that leadership lasts forever without nurture.

This is the kind of mistake that today's foodservice professionals cannot afford to make. The foodservice industry caters to one of the most primal, and unchangeable, of human needs. It is particularly susceptible to rapid market obsolescence—especially if it practices marshmallow marketing that can either block its vision or tie its hands.

With this in mind, look again at the list of seven marshmallow marketing alarms and, on a scale of 0 to 7, rate your organization on each item. (A 0 would mark you as fault-free and a 7 as in terrific trouble.)

Since you've answered honestly, and you've started to gain a marketing perspective, you'll be able to evaluate the results honestly yourself. If you've scored any one item 3 or above, you've got something to worry about. You need to act on it seriously and quickly. If you've scored a number of items 3 or above, you have much remedial marketing to do. And, if you've scored a perfect 0—well, maybe you need to question your honesty or your perception, because nobody's perfect.

What it all comes down to is this: In foodservice, you have to emulate General Patton and be ready to shoot the mules—in other words, take care of the details.

MARKETING AN ATTITUDE

When you come right down to it, foodservice markets an attitude. To make this apparent to all of the people in a foodservice chain, I designed an experiment at a one-day workshop that culminated in an evening banquet. One-third of the tables were given poor service. Forks were missing, coffee was cold, meringue from the lemon pie was on the water glasses, water glasses were filled so full that when you picked them up they would spill. The waiters and waitresses were told to be moderately inattentive and sometimes rude. Workshop participants were randomly assigned to the tables. The modified service had each participant pick up a plate of food that was the same for everyone. The experiment was a secret.

The chain's vice president for sales happened to sit at a table with poor service. When he sipped his coffee, it was cold. So he called, "Waitress, my coffee's cold." She picked up the pot, patted it, and said, "That's funny, because the pot's hot," and walked away. That's poor service (and, unfortunately, not all that unusual).

At the conclusion of the evening, each participant rated all aspects of the day's seminar. The results: People who had poor service rated the city where the convention was held, the convention center, and the presentation lower than those who had good service. Each of the items on the plate was listed for evaluation, and the greatest variance in rating between the people who had good and poor service was the tastiness of the meat.

Food is an attitude. Consumers are attracted to restaurants with winning attitudes. Managers and co-workers make a great difference in the attitudes in a restaurant, and success is the result of having an attitude that wins customers.

CHAPTER HIGHLIGHTS AND REVIEW

1) Plans based on inaccurate and inadequate information are doomed to fail. Know your customers and your competition.

2) Overlooking the obvious by focusing too narrowly on your business and not on its surrounding environment leads to missed opportunities.

3) Weak or nonquantifiable goals tend to direct your activities toward mediocrity or, worse yet, failure.

4) A mixed-up set of marketing mix components creates confusion, and, in some cases, pure chaos.

5) Poor follow-through means you may never know what worked, what didn't work, and why.

6) If you forget the basic purpose of promotion—to generate traffic—in favor of building your image, your promotions are doomed.

7) If every key member of your strategic business unit isn't totally informed of your marketing plans, chances are that plan execution will be ineffective.

8) Foodservice markets an attitude. It's up to you whether the attitude is positive or negative.

Chapter Three

25 Reasons Why You Need the Right Marketing Plan

Success in a foodservice operation depends on four essential ingredients:

- A restaurant concept oriented to real customer needs and executed with dedication to excellence
- A marketing organization that effectively attracts customers to try the concept
- A customer-responsive service and operations staff
- A marketing plan that identifies the target audience, sets strategies, and assigns responsibilities for implementing action programs to achieve specific desired results

The last of these ingredients, the marketing plan, is by far the most important. Although the four ingredients obviously depend on one another, it is the proper execution of the marketing plan that in the majority of cases determines the optimal profitability of any foodservice venture. And, as the strength of the marketing plan dictates the extent of success, its weaknesses determine the depth of failure.

To put this in another light, the finest restaurant concept is almost certainly doomed without a marketing organization and a marketing plan to breathe life into it. A marketing organization with impressive credentials cannot compensate for a weak plan or a questionable concept. Customer responsiveness is indispensable; a planning framework will ensure its consistency. A skillfully devised marketing plan can influence, and even rescue for a short time, the shaky concept or the relatively inexperienced marketing group.

How can a marketing plan help you? The correctly crafted marketing plan will enable you to:

- Give your organization a set track to run on
- Create a stable, planning-oriented framework
- Encourage and facilitate organized thinking
- Pinpoint strengths and weaknesses
- Analyze your competitors
- Place potential in the proper perspective
- Expose hidden obstacles
- Identify hidden opportunities
- Rank priorities realistically
- Isolate problems and effective solutions
- Select specific targets
- Point the way toward directed creativity
- Coordinate and strengthen all marketing tools
- Evaluate alternative strategies
- Set target dates and deadlines
- Formalize accountability and responsibility for results
- Remove guesswork from budgeting
- Maintain aim on profitability
- Pave the way for growth
- Institute meaningful review criteria to measure progress
- Prepare for corrective action in the event of variances
- Lay a foundation for followup planning
- Strengthen employee and management motivation and teamwork
- Improve organizational procedures
- Create action rather than reaction

A sound marketing plan is indispensable to foodservice survival, success, and competitive supremacy. It is an axiom of the industry that a sound marketing plan underlies all successful marketing activities. You'll lose out if you just wait around for ideas to materialize rather than plan to make things happen and to win.

The most obvious advantage of a sound marketing plan is that it provides you with a document aimed squarely at specific results within the framework of a defined marketing environment. You can have all the ideas in the world, but until you formalize them in a plan that you can communicate throughout your entire organization, you have nothing.

Consequently, the winning marketing plan is always written out clearly and is based on internal and external data that have been carefully collected and analyzed to avoid bias or error. It should tell you who you really are, where you are going, and how you're going to get there. Your plan should spell out exactly how you intend to marshal your resources to attack carefully chosen marketing targets. It should creatively combine the marketing mix variables into a systematic, integrated array of strategies that effectively differentiate between opportunity and threat and tell you how to address both in ways that are operationally feasible.

But you don't create a disciplined plan without a disciplined process. (See Figure 3.1 for the marketing plan development flow.) The validity of the plan depends on the validity of the process. Moreover, the process itself is educative in a way that is extremely difficult to duplicate. What you, your marketing organization in general, and the rest of the entire operation learn about the realities of your foodservice company should serve you well for years to come. Properly executed, the process should produce invaluable information about the real workings of your business. Beyond that, it will have a lasting, positive impact on the way the people in your company think about your business—and their thinking will become increasingly disciplined and keyed to marketing.

It's very easy to be complacent about your marketing plan. Many foodservice providers ignore the basics. Their marketing plan does not keep them focused properly; their plan, with all its trappings and fancy covers, deludes the company into thinking that its marketing is just as good as it can be.

To provide a further focus on marketing dynamics, consider this: Although your marketing plan will encompass many subsidiary objectives, an increase in profits is its ultimate goal. Increased profits primarily depend on increased sales, cost containment notwithstanding. And, there are only three ways to increase sales:

1) Increase customer traffic by adding more units, reaching untapped segments of your market, increasing group size, taking customers from your competition, and adding services (e.g., providing catering).

2) Increase frequency of customer visits by generating bounceback from one part of the day to another, adding more variety to your menu, and providing special reasons for increased visits (e.g., punch cards).

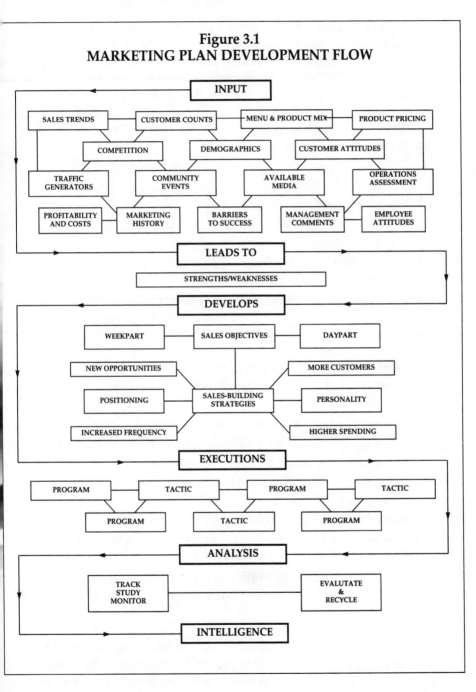

Figure 3.1
MARKETING PLAN DEVELOPMENT FLOW

3) Increase average check size by adding higher priced menu items, increasing prices, selling add-ons to your meals, bundling menu items, and exercising profitable positioning of menu items.

Your key task as a marketer is to find the right ways to do all of the above better than your competition.

To accomplish this, you must develop a marketing plan, a process that includes seven basic action steps:

- Collecting base data
- Identifying strengths and weaknesses
- Stating specific objectives
- Developing marketing strategies
- Developing and executing tactical programs
- Establishing budgets and timetables
- Putting in place measurements and controls for evaluating results

You should ask yourself some questions at this point:

- What needs does my market have now, and how can I satisfy them?
- How can I differentiate my market offering from those of the competition?
- What is the most effective timing for my marketing efforts?
- What is the current and projected demand for my concept?
- What, precisely, is my competitive environment?
- What are the basic strengths of my concept and format and how can they be improved?
- Who are my target customers? Are they the right targets?
- How effective is my organization in executing the format at the unit level?
- How efficient and effective is my current marketing effort?
- Do I have the financial and human resources I need to support my marketing effort?

To that last question, an important corollary must be appended: *Are you operationally ready for your marketing plan?* No matter how "psyched up" you may be about marketing or how much effort you put into developing a plan, you will not attain maximum results unless you are well prepared operationally. As a matter of fact, the marketing program can backfire

Figure 3.2
COMPETITIVE EVALUATION FORM

Location _____   Date of Evaluation _____

Evaluator _____

First rate your location (using the codes below), then rate your competitors compared to your location in each of the following categories. Add any additional categories you feel are pertinent (i.e., entertainment or cover charges for a lounge). Indicate in the marketing opportunities column any areas in which you hold a competitive advantage.

Competitor's Name

My Location | Marketing Opportunities | Competitors Overall

CATEGORY										
MENU VARIETY										
MENU APPEAL										
FOOD/BEVERAGE QUALITY										
FOOD/BEVERAGE TASTE										
FOOD/BEVERAGE CONSISTENCY										
PORTION SIZE										
PRICING										
SERVICE SPEED										
SERVICE QUALITY										
SERVICE FRIENDLINESS										
CLEANLINESS										
PROMOTIONAL ACTIVITY										
VISIBILITY										
IMAGE										
ATMOSPHERE										
FACILITY										
SALES LEVEL										
POINT OF SALE										
HAPPY HOUR OFFERINGS										

My Location: E = Excellent   G = Good   F = Fair   P = Poor

Competitors: MB = Much Better   B = Better   S = Similar   W = Worse   MW = Much Worse

Comments/Explanations: _____

completely if unit-level operations are not up to handling it. As true as that is in any organization, it is even more critical in foodservice, where marketing and operations are closely related in so many areas.

In foodservice, whatever is planned from the marketing perspective must be worked out and implemented operationally as well. In fact, as any need for operational changes and improvements becomes evident during the marketing planning process, that need should be addressed. If you find that your service is slow or your units need renovation, you should correct such situations immediately—and certainly prior to the implementation of new marketing programs.

It's foolish to introduce a new menu item using extensive promotions designed to increase traffic if your restrooms are shabby, there are potholes in the parking lot, or production is not up to par. The new customers, brought in through promotion, may love the new item, but they will also be introduced to aspects of your operation that will repel them—maybe permanently. This is why operational improvement is an important aspect of the process.

Before entering into the marketing plan process itself, you will find it very valuable to have your unit operators complete the competitive evaluation form shown in Figure 3.2. To do this properly and objectively, they will have to "shop" the competition, an activity that should, at any rate, be encouraged as a regular responsibility.

You will find that by copying the form and having the copies completed by your local managers now, you can put them on notice that you are starting a new planning process and are insisting on their cooperation. As difficult as it may be, you must insist on complete objectivity when your managers rate their own operations. The "My Restaurant" portion of the rating sheet forms the basis for meaningful competitive comparison, and it needs to be as pure as possible. Accurate self-grading is absolutely necessary. It's a good idea to have each of your employees fill out the competitive evaluation form.

Once these forms have been filled out properly and reviewed, managers will gain a new view of their operations, and you will gain a new perspective on all of your operations that will provide a context for your planning.

CHAPTER HIGHLIGHTS AND REVIEW

1) A skillfully devised marketing plan should not only satisfy your short-term needs, but also contribute to the building and maintenance of your concept's longer-term positioning and success.

2) There are, at the very least, 25 ways a marketing plan can help you. Remember them and use them.

3) Your plan should spell out exactly how you intend to marshal your resources to attack carefully chosen marketing targets.

4) There are only three ways to build sales volume: build customer traffic; increase purchase frequency by your current customers; and build average per customer expenditure. These are your key marketing strategies. Use them independently or in combination.

5) You will not optimize your plan's potential unless you are operationally ready for the customers you attract.

6) The competitive evaluation form will give you a view of your absolute strengths and weaknesses, of your position relative to your competition.

7) The marketing plan development flow chart illustrates the areas that must be considered in structuring an effective plan.

Chapter Four

Know Thy Customers and Know Them Well

The structuring of your marketing plan starts with collection of base data. There are certain kinds of data that you should be, and very probably are, already gathering more or less regularly.

For most of you, this chapter should be a review—a review with some very serious purposes. The first of these, in order of logic if not importance, is to focus your concentration on aspects of research approach and methodology that the press of business may be causing you and your staff to overlook, much to the detriment of your marketing effort. A second purpose is to help you fill in any gaps in base data collection by suggesting some important information areas that may currently be neglected by your organization. A third aim is to provide you with some well-defined methods of data collection that should be pursued as you start your marketing plan. A series of worksheets reenforces the kind of disciplined thinking that will give you the foundation you will need to create a sound marketing plan.

You will notice that the word "research" has occurred only once so far in this chapter, referring primarily to data collection even though the terms are largely interchangeable. This avoids evoking the reflexive reaction to research that sometimes develops among marketing professionals. Research is essential, they frequently tell themselves, but it is complicated, time-consuming, and costly—and "after all, I'm smart enough to anticipate instinctively a lot of what research is going to tell me." Of course, research is essential, but it only becomes complicated, time-consuming, and costly because some marketers insist on making it so.

Properly carried out, research yields information that serves as a check on the respective marketplace position held by you and your competitors. It should be an invaluable data resource no matter what corporate enterprise you are confronting: adding or expanding units; changing your menu; amending your budget; revising your product line, or taking a new approach to marketing plan development.

There are many data collection methodologies applicable at varying levels in a restaurant organization. Obviously, the size and type of your organization dictate the nature and extent of the program you should conduct. Large regional or national concepts require broad-scale research efforts and specialized expertise to design and handle extensive and sophisticated projects. Smaller chains may also use an outside firm if their budgets permit, although they will find that they can conduct meaningful research very profitably and economically.

No matter which situation best describes your organization, you will find the methods presented in this book extremely useful—either in pursuing your own research or in enhancing the foodservice-specific direction you can give to an outside firm or to your internal support groups.

Many research efforts in the foodservice industry go awry, simply because the foodservice company or the research firm it had engaged ignored a basic industry truth: All valid research (and, therefore, all valid market planning) must *start* and *end* with the living, breathing, eating customers in each trading area—and even contiguous trading areas can differ dramatically.

Consequently, regardless of the size of the foodservice firm, locally conducted, unit-level research is imperative. No matter how large your organization, you must test the pulse of the actual person who enters your establishment—or perhaps will not enter it again. You can attain the type of information you need for success in foodservice only by contact with customers at the unit level.

A large foodservice organization that relies only on broad-based indicators and research results is missing out on some of the best "research data" available and probably paying far too much for amassing the data it is receiving for analysis—data that may have very questionable value.

A brief digression on some research you can pursue for yourself seems in order here. For instance, a large family-owned supermarket in the Northeast attributes its high volume to customer loyalty. They talk constantly with their customers and are ready to respond to their suggestions and needs. Their prime communications vehicle: do-it-yourself discussion groups. Every Saturday morning, the owners meet with a group of customers to discuss new and better ways to do business. The owners listen and act—and all their customers are aware of this. In another instance, a large restaurant chain recruits customers for a biweekly focus session. Ongoing dialogue keeps the chain's decision makers in touch with customers. Do you know what your customers are saying about *your* prices, *your* products, about the business that is *your* livelihood?

Focus groups need not be structured by outside consultants and interpreted to a fare-thee-well and beyond the time that the results will be most useful. And, you need not pay a lot of money or spend a lot of time getting information that is at best nebulous.

Remember that the purpose of a focus group is to get reaction, feelings, direction, and subjective commentary from a group of consumers to help in decision making. Focus groups provide no statistically valid information, no numbers, no percentages, no averages—just a sense of whether or not you're on the right track. This sense, sharpened by attention, can be very helpful in developing new products, menus, advertising, and decor. It may even give new life to your operation or present a never-thought-of-before way to please your customers.

Do-it-yourself focus groups mean just that: no one-way observation glass, just a group of your people affably talking to your customers—customers who will enjoy the pipeline to management.

Another simple, internally oriented research method that offers reliable results at reasonable costs is the core store panel. The purpose of a core store restaurant panel is to provide corporate headquarters with local information from a representative sample of stores on a timely and continuing basis. A core store panel should be implemented by closely following these steps:

1) Store selection
2) Data collection
3) Analysis
4) Data report

Step 1: Store Selection. The core store panel makeup should match the chain's makeup. Stores on the panel should have geographical representation aligning with chain distribution by region. If 10 percent of the stores in the chain are located in the Northeast, for example, 10 percent of the stores on the core store panel should be located in the Northeast. Core store panel members should also have sales representative of the region. That is, if 30 percent of the stores in the region are classified as "high sales" stores, 50 percent are classified as "average sales" stores, and 20 percent are classified as "low sales" stores, the stores selected to participate in the core store panel should represent these percentages. All core store panel member stores should be in full operational compliance.

Of course, cooperative managers are a must.

Step 2: Data Collection. While the kind of information that can be obtained from a core store panel is almost endless, the most important information is:

- Sales by day/week
- Transaction count
- Product sales mix
- Advertising activities
- Promotional activities
- Competitive activities
- Weather

Coordinators will obtain data weekly, via telephone or fax, utilizing a standard form/questionnaire.

Step 3: Analysis. The data obtained from a core store panel will be analyzed immediately after they are gathered by appropriate corporate personnel.

Step 4: Data Report. The information obtained from a core store panel should be compiled on a monthly basis and a formal report prepared for presentation to management oversight committees.

Of course, great care must be exercised in communicating unit-level results to those who are in a position to make major marketing decisions. Often the real message to be conveyed gets lost in transmission, possibly because someone at the unit level feels the need to protect or project personal ideas, to guard against territorial invasion, or to cover up incompetence. This problem can be overcome if adequate communications mechanisms are in place throughout the organization.

For instance, a unit-level representative can be designated to report directly to staff management, serving as a constant liaison between unit-level operations and decision makers. An alternative would be for staff management to make it a consistent practice to visit units and to talk with unit-level staff. These two methods have the added benefit of creating and preserving a two-way communications channel that could be of inestimable value to the organization. Deployed in tandem, they could become a powerful information tool. No matter what communications technique is used, staff managers should not overlook the truly critical necessity of remaining in continuing and reliable contact with field staff—and, through the field staff, with the all-important customer.

SELECTING THE OUTSIDE RESEARCH FIRM

Depending on the nature and extent of your research requirements, your staffing and budget limitations, and the size and complexity of your operation, you may wish to seek professional outside research assistance.

You can use a research firm in several ways: to provide guidance for your own efforts; to handle certain aspects of your research or analysis; or to undertake the entire project.

Choosing the right research firm can seem an even more formidable task than the research itself. Beware: There are research amateurs who masquerade as professionals and who can cause you trouble, cost you money, and damage your business. Solid answers to the following questions, however, should help you in your quest for a reliable professional firm:

1) How long has the research firm been in business? Can they refer you to other clients?

2) Who of the firm's principals and staff will be assigned to your project? What percentage of their time will be allocated to your needs? What is their experience in general? What is their specific experience in the foodservice industry?

3) Does the firm's proposal indicate accurate understanding of your research needs? Does the proposal contain costly statistical "bells and whistles" or down-to-earth approaches that are comprehensible and usable?

4) Is the firm's timetable reasonable and realistic?

5) Are the estimated costs reasonable in relation to the assignment?

6) Can the firm demonstrate the analytical skills needed to interpret foodservice data correctly? Perhaps you can set up a "test" of these skills by providing the firm with previously collected data and asking for an interpretation that will give you a good idea of the firm's foodservice sensibilities.

You should entertain proposals from at least three firms to compare values and approaches, as well as to learn more about the entire research process yourself.

MARKET RESEARCH: THE HOW-TO PRINCIPLES

Research goals, questions, and methods must be decided on in advance to ensure that your research tells you what you really need to know. The basic sequence of market research should be:

- Develop research objectives.
- Decide on questions to be answered or specific information to be uncovered.
- Select the most appropriate research methodology.
- Conduct the research.

This chapter includes three questionnaires/worksheets to be used in conducting unit-level customer research at restaurants. As you will see, they are designed to reveal just how your customers really feel about your restaurant, to provide ratings on aspects of your operation, and to tell you where your current customers come from. Later, you will learn how to interpret this information and put it to work for your restaurant.

A word on survey design: When you look at a survey question, make sure that the answer will help you to make a decision. Research is undertaken to eliminate uncertainties, so you will want to make sure that a question will produce a usable answer—but not a biased one. Before executing the questions, write down what answers might be elicited and what decisions they might commit you to. Avoid asking questions that only raise other questions and leave you without focus. Anticipate the answers and redesign the question until it gives you the kind of answer you can use. Finally, don't be afraid to pretest a survey. A trial run on a small sample of respondents will help in the process of spotting and refining weak questions and building in backups.

THE CAP STUDY

The first questionnaire is a customer attitude profile (CAP) study. Ideally, you should survey around 10 percent of your customer base to obtain a reliable sampling of attitudes, preferences, perceptions, and distribution. Participants should be interviewed over a typical four-day period that represents all facets of customer traffic. For most operations, Thursday to Sunday interviewing is recommended.

Figure 4.1
CUSTOMER ATTITUDE PROFILE STUDY

Hello, my name is _____, and I'd like to ask you a few short questions about your experience at this restaurant. It will only take about three minutes. Would you mind helping us out?

		1	2	3	4	5	6	7
1.	How often do you come here?	Once a week or more	Two to three times a month	Once a month	Less than one time a month	First visit		
2.	How often do you eat at this type of restaurant?	Once a week or more	Two to three times a month	Once a month	Less than one time a month	First visit		
3.	Are you a . . .	Local resident	Local worker	Seasonal resident	Tourist	Other		
4.	How long did it take you to get here?	Under 5 minutes	5 – 10 minutes	11 – 15 minutes	16 – 25 minutes	25 + minutes		
5.	Where did you just come from prior to visiting today?	Shopping	Home	Work	School	Recreation	Other	
6.	Where do you plan to go after leaving this restaurant?	Shopping	Home	Work	School	Recreation	Other	
7.	Including you, how many people are you buying food for?	One	Two	Three	Four	Five or more		
8.	Including you, how many people are you with today?	One	Two	Three	Four	Five or more		
9.	What are your TWO main reasons for coming?	Recommendation	Passing by	Ad/Coupon	Convenience	Food	View	Other

10. What other restaurants nearby do you eat at most often? (List in order of frequency - using #1 as most frequent.)

    1._____   2._____   3._____

           4._____   5._____

11. On a scale of 1 to 5, with 5 being excellent, how would you rate our restaurant on the following:

		Excellent	Good	Average	Fair	Poor
11.1	Food	5	4	3	2	1
11.2	Service	5	4	3	2	1
11.3	Friendliness	5	4	3	2	1
11.4	Prices	5	4	3	2	1
11.5	Overall Rating	5	4	3	2	1

Interviews should be conducted from opening to closing to achieve a representation of your customer base over all hours of operation. This is extremely important since the characteristics of your customer base will undoubtedly change drastically according to the time of day they patronize the restaurant. Ten percent of your customer base for all meal periods should be covered. The CAP questionnaire is shown in Figure 4.1.

A few recommendations on interviewing approach and technique are in order. First, interviewers should not wear any restaurant uniforms or identification. Otherwise customers may suppress negative comments—

12. Now, please rate us again, but this time compare us to #1 in question 10 above:

	Much Better	Better	Similar	Worse	Much Worse
11.1 Food	5	4	3	2	1
11.2 Service	5	4	3	2	1
11.3 Friendliness	5	4	3	2	1
11.4 Prices	5	4	3	2	1
11.5 Overall Rating	5	4	3	2	1

13. Is there any reason you might not visit us again? Please tell us so we can correct any problems:

_____

_____

14. Could you please tell us your Zip Code for: Home _____ Work _____

That's all - Thank you very much. You've been very helpful.

Interviewer observe and circle:

15. Gender:	1 Male	2 Female					
16. Age:	1 18 – 24	2 25 – 34	3 35 – 49	4 50 – 64	5 65+		
17. Ethnicity:	1 Black	2 Caucasian	3 Hispanic	4 Other			
18. Today is:	1 Mon.	2 Tues.	3 Wed.	4 Thurs.	5 Fri.	6 Sat.	7 Sun.
19. Time:	1 Open – 11 AM	2 11 AM – 4 PM	3 4 PM – Close				
20. Meal for:	1 Dine-in	2 Take-out	3 Drive-thru				

and you certainly want to hear these. The image projected should be one of impartiality. Street clothes are preferable, but should be as "dressy" as possible to signal the seriousness of the interview. Interviewers should be instructed not to approach the customer with a question that can be answered yes or no. A question such as "Excuse me, do you have a few minutes?" gives customers time to decide that they don't really want to cooperate and provides an opening to refuse quickly. Instead, the interviewer should open by saying, "Hello, my name is _____, and I'd like to ask you a few short questions about your experience at this restaurant. It will only take about three minutes. Will you help us, please?"

The interviewer must keep the interview as brief as possible and not introduce any incidental conversation that could give the customer a chance to terminate the interview prematurely and invalidate all previous responses. The interview should be conducted after the customer has finished eating.

Figure 4.2
MYSTERY SHOPPER RESEARCH EVALUATION

Date _____   Restaurant Location/Unit Number _____

Time Started _____   Time Completed _____

EXTERIOR AND SIGNAGE	EXCELLENT	VERY GOOD	GOOD	FAIR	POOR
Parking Lot Cleanliness	____	____	____	____	____
Sidewalk Cleanliness	____	____	____	____	____
Window Cleanliness	____	____	____	____	____
Working Order of Outside Signs	____	____	____	____	____
Cleanliness/Neatness of Inside Signs	____	____	____	____	____
Visibility of Point of Purchase Signs	____	____	____	____	____

INTERIOR	EXCELLENT	VERY GOOD	GOOD	FAIR	POOR
General Appearance of Eating Area	____	____	____	____	____
Cleanliness of Eating Area	____	____	____	____	____
Cleanliness of Restrooms	____	____	____	____	____
Availability of Soap, Towels, etc.	____	____	____	____	____

STAFF APPEARANCE	EXCELLENT	VERY GOOD	GOOD	FAIR	POOR
Manager	____	____	____	____	____
Wait Staff	____	____	____	____	____
Counter Staff	____	____	____	____	____

STAFF PERFORMANCE	EXCELLENT	VERY GOOD	GOOD	FAIR	POOR
Friendliness of Staff	____	____	____	____	____
Efficiency of Staff	____	____	____	____	____

SERVICE	NOT APPLICABLE	NO	YES
Was your order repeated for verification?	_____	____	____
Were your questions answered politely?	_____	____	____
Did the Counter/Wait Person suggest you purchase any additional items?	_____	____	____
Were the tables left unclean for more than a few minutes?	_____	____	____
Were your items served as ordered?	_____	____	____

Page 2

SERVICE (Continued)

How long did you wait for your food/beverage after your order was taken?

    Less than 5 minutes?   _____

    5 - 10 minutes?   _____

    10 - 15 minutes?   _____

Estimate the number of customers in the restaurant when you received your order:

    1 - 5   _____

    6 - 10   _____

    11 - 20   _____

    21 - 30   _____

    31 or more   _____

Enter any additional comments or observations about the restaurant, service, prices, or menu:

_____

_____

_____

_____

_____

_____

THE MYSTERY SHOPPER

Another part of a fundamental consumer research program is the time-honored "mystery shopper method." You can either contact a professional shopper service to conduct the "mystery shopper" research or you can have local residents complete an evaluation form. (In the early nineties, shopper service firms typically charged a per visit fee of $45, plus the price of the meal and tip, if any.) You may find that local residents will simply charge you for the meal and tip.

Whether you arrange for local help or engage a firm, these suggestions should be useful:

- The shopper should remain anonymous, even after the visit.
- Evaluation times should be random, but should occur during the commonly defined meal periods.
- Evaluation should be conducted three or four times the first month, and once a month subsequently.
- Don't act on the reports until several have been submitted. Remember that it is possible to have a totally different restaurant experience during the same day as shifts change.

The mystery shopper evaluation form is shown in Figure 4.2.

ZIP CODE/TRADING AREA IDENTIFICATION

Zip code information, properly compiled and interpreted, will give shape and definition to your restaurant's trading area. Zip code data will mark out those areas in which you can most effectively direct marketing efforts, and in many cases, will show where your customers come from and where customers are *not* coming from, possibly exposing untapped pockets of potential business.

The first step in this exercise is to obtain a map of the restaurant's immediate environs that includes postal zip codes and boundaries. A call to your local post office may be a helpful starting point.

Once the map is in hand, a customer zip code record (see Figure 4.3) should be kept. The actual collection of the zip code data will be performed by restaurant servers and cashiers. Have table servers ask customers to record their home and work zip codes on the guest check,

Figure 4.3
CUSTOMER ZIP CODE RECORD

Location _____

Date _____

I.   Record area zip codes across the top (in numerical order)

II. Ask customers for their home zip codes

III. Place a check in the column beneath the zip code where they live.

Zip Codes																				Out of Area	No Response

Figure 4.4
ZIP CODE DATA CONSOLIDATION SHEET

LOCATION _____ DATE _____

MEAL PERIOD _____

Zip Code	#	:	Zip Code	#	:
Out of Area					
No Response					

or have counter servers enter zip code information they obtain by questioning customers on copies of the record. For the most reliable results, zip code collection should be conducted over a two-week period. A reasonably accurate sample of customer zip codes can be obtained, however, by using a four-day period. One person in the restaurant should be given the responsibility of coordinating the information and compiling it on the Zip Code Data Consolidation Sheet (Figure 4.4). When the consolidation has been completed, you will have a clear indication of what percentage of your customers *lives* in each zip code, as well as what percentage *works* in each zip code area.

SUPPLEMENTAL KNOW THY CUSTOMERS AND KNOW THEM WELL TECHNIQUES

There are, of course, less formal research techniques that can be used to complement the information and impressions obtained using the questionnaires/worksheets. They should *not* be substituted for the disciplined approach of the questionnaires/worksheets!

The first of these techniques is to talk to customers informally, but in line with the directions taken in the questionnaires. The ambience in some restaurants is conducive to conversation. The result of these talks may not be hard, usable facts, but a personal sense of what lies behind the facts.

The second supplemental approach is customer comment cards (see Figure 4.5). Cards yield more responses than conversations. Cards can focus on troublesome questionnaire responses. They can be changed from time to time, perhaps seasonally. In the spring, for example, your card could concentrate on customer service; in the summer, you could solicit comment on menu items; in the fall, questions could focus on convenience and accessibility.

Several caveats are in order at this point. First, methods of properly analyzing the information gathered will be discussed later in this book. Until that point, don't pick out isolated pieces of information and make important marketing decisions based on them. Other data collection areas could throw a completely different light on some of those bits and pieces. Second, remember that in-store research has a positive bias built in. Unless customers have a real complaint, they are not likely to come up with negative comments. In short, extremely positive results must be discounted to some extent.

Figure 4.5
SAMPLE COMMENT CARD

RECEIPT

Date________ Food & Bar________

Gratuity________

Guests________ TOTAL________

We invite your comments...

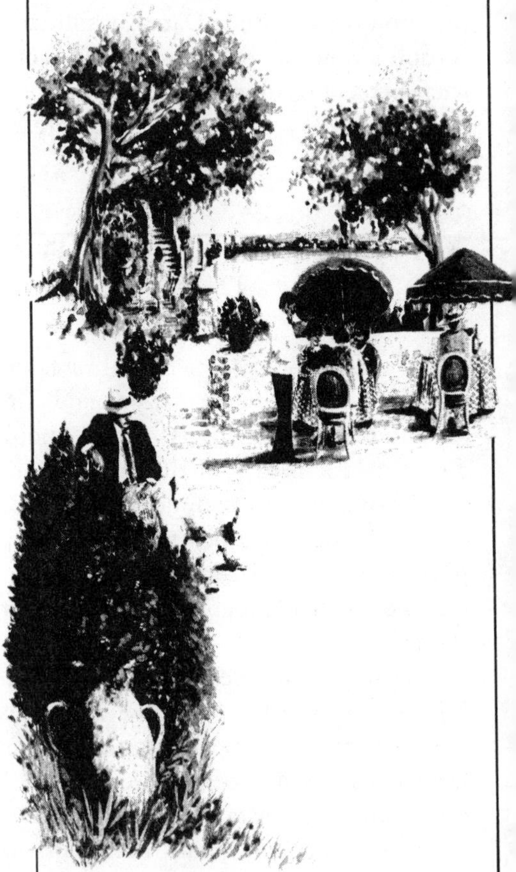

the Olive Garden®
ITALIAN RESTAURANT

Parties to Go!

Delicious Olive Garden entrees, salad & breadsticks and desserts. The convenient way to make your next party, picnic or any kind of get-together a treat for everyone.

Call us.
We'll have your Parties to Go order ready for pick-up when you want it.

A LA CARTE ENTREES (in heat'n serve containers)		
Lasagna	Serves up to 12	$25.00
Cheese Ravioli	Serves up to 10	$28.00
Beef Ravioli	Serves up to 10	$30.00
Manicotti	Serves up to 10	$27.00
Cannelloni	Serves up to 8	$27.00
Spaghetti w/Meat Sauce	Serves up to 16	$20.00
Spaghetti w/Sausage or Meatballs	Serves up to 12	$30.00
SALAD & BREADSTICKS		
Jumbo Garden Salad w/ a dozen Breadsticks	Serves 5-6	$ 8.00
Breadsticks, per dozen		$ 2.50
DESSERTS		
Cheesecake	Serves 12	$25.00
Chocolate Mousse Pie	Serves 12	$25.00
Zuppa Inglese	Serves 12	$25.00

Choose any of the above Parties to Go, or any items from our great tasting menu.

Our management staff will be happy to help you solve your full range of dining needs...

- Restaurant accommodations for large parties.
- Olive Garden gift certificates

Please let us know how you feel...

Our managers and staff are here to serve you. Would you please take a moment to jot down how you feel, and drop this card in the comment box near our front door. If you require anything further, feel free to contact us at:

The Olive Garden Customer Relations
P.O. Box 592037
Orlando, FL 32859-2037

Thanks for dining with us. *Arrivederci!*

1. *Your visit with us today:* Date_____
   location/city_____
   ❏ lunch ❏ dinner number in your party____

2. *How often do you eat at The Olive Garden?*
   ❏ first time ❏ once in a while ❏ regularly

3. *Tell us about your meal:*
   food taste:
   excellent ⑥ ⑤ ④ ③ ② ① poor
   comments _____
   _____

4. *How was our lobby staff?*
   excellent ⑥ ⑤ ④ ③ ② ① poor

5. *Tell us about your server:*
   (name/# _____):
   excellent ⑥ ⑤ ④ ③ ② ① poor

6. *How do our prices compare to food and service?*
   ❏about right ❏lower than expected
   ❏overpriced

7. *What do you like most/least about us?*
   most_____
   least_____

8. *How do you feel overall about your visit?*
   highly satisfied ⑥ ⑤ ④ ③ ② ① dissatisfied

9. Your name_____
   address_____
   city_____ state_____
   zip_____ phone_____

Figure 4.5 (*continued*)

CHAPTER HIGHLIGHTS AND REVIEW

1) Do you have an ongoing research program in place, giving you data about your customers' buying habits and about their perceptions of your business?

2) Is someone in your organization responsible for managing this vital data-gathering function?

3) When was the last time you had an anonymous shopper visit your outlet to report on the purchase experience from a customer's perspective? How often do you conduct this type of research?

4) Are you equipped with data that reveal the geographic distribution of each location's customer base? By meal period? By weekpart?

5) Do you have a program calling for location personnel to conduct informal customer research, providing feedback for your marketing decision making?

6) Remember these seven key research methods:

Do-It-Yourself Discussion Groups

Core Store Panels

Customer Attitude Profile

Mystery Shopper

Zip Code/Trading Area Identification

Informal Discussion

Customer Comment Card

Chapter Five

The ATUs of Consumer Habits = the ABCs of Your Business

Successful, productive consumer research, the type that will enable you to create a sound foodservice marketing plan, is a multilevel, interrelated process. To leave out one research component is to risk replacing success with failure.

It is essential that you gain an understanding of the consumer market you serve based on trends in the key consumer criteria of awareness/trial/ usage (ATU) attitudes and demographics. Monitoring these trends will exponentially increase your understanding of your consumer market, including customers and noncustomers, and will enable you to more clearly delineate your market and its basic structure and to harness the dynamics that drive consumer patronage and preferences. This knowledge will enable you to make well-informed decisions, to draw up action plans, and to create opportunity from threat.

The information you gain from an ongoing consumer tracking study will permit you to develop marketing programs based on knowledge of your position versus the position of your competition, to refine and redirect expansion plans, and to conceptualize and implement product and service offerings that rank high in the value scale. It feeds directly into positioning strategies and into developing your brand personality.

With all this buildup, you may be asking yourself, "What's the catch?" And your instincts are right. There is a catch that those instincts probably have already defined for you. Consumer tracking information is highly sophisticated and you really need to engage specialists to do it for you.

The specialists I recommend to my clients are Michele Schmal and Bob

Siegel, principals of Restaurant Consulting Group (RCG), Inc., in Evanston, Illinois. They have been extremely successful in identifying and quantifying clients' market position (strengths and weaknesses) across markets and versus competition through use of consumer research.

I am indebted to RCG for their permission to use some portions of their material as the basis of some of the fundamental definitions and descriptions of the rationale and technique involved in consumer tracking.

RCG's approach assumes the measurement of the number of people visiting your units as critical. That number—the size of your customer base—comprises three components: awareness, trial, and repeat usage.

Awareness is defined as the percent of people in your "interested universe" who have heard of your restaurant. Awareness depends largely on your competitive presence, on the length of time you've been in the market, and on the extent to which advertising, public relations, and word-of-mouth reputation combine to bring your restaurant to the attention of consumers.

Trial reflects the number of "aware" people (cumulatively) who have ever visited or ordered from your restaurant. The prime factors here are the quality and quantity of unit distribution, the effectiveness of your appeal, and communication and consumer differentiation of benefits/ expectations versus alternative restaurant choices.

Repeat usage represents the number of people who have tried your restaurant and who return on a regular, current basis. Repeat visits depend largely on delivery of products and services matched against consumer expectations. Promotion and menu enhancements also encourage return visits.

Consumer tracking consists essentially of using the way awareness, trial, and repeat usage relate to each other across markets or over time— the ratios of conversion—to compute the actual size of your customer base. Since some current customers make only one visit during a given period—say a month—while others make 20 visits, it is important to calculate the average frequency of visit per customer.

A word of caution is essential here. The single most important error made by foodservice chain management is to regard average visit frequency as the prime determinant of chain "health" or "success." All too often, you hear, "Our visit frequency has improved from 3.0 to 3.5 visits per month—we must be doing a good job of satisfying our customers." That conclusion may be totally invalid, as you will notice in Figure 5.1, where the average number of visits for Period 1 is 3.0 compared to 3.5 for Period 2. However, the customer count for Period 1 is 90, compared to 84 for Period 2.

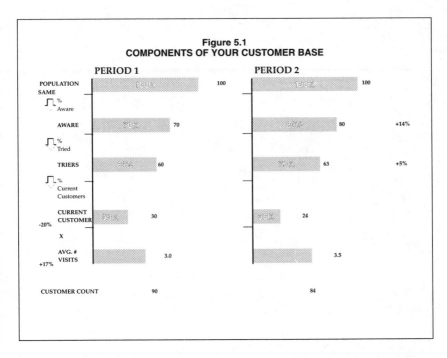

Figure 5.1
COMPONENTS OF YOUR CUSTOMER BASE

A more appropriate use of these measures would be to quantify, compare, and trend them for your organization and your important competitors as the foundation for systemwide action plans and programs. You should also be able to use this information to develop programs for specific markets or market types. In other words, you should be able to set strategies with confidence and then create tactical plans to exploit individual markets, plans that recognize the differences in customer base structure.

Using structural information to determine an appropriate program approach for differing circumstances is illustrated in Figure 5.2.

Typically, a consumer research plan would extend considerably beyond identifying and quantifying these elements of consumer behavior to providing demographic information and measuring and evaluating the "diagnostics" driving various behavior patterns. The demographics will be used primarily as background for store placement and for targeting advertising programs. The diagnostics will be employed to clarify answers to the "Why" questions inherent in analyzing the "Who, How Many, How Often" elements of the research.

It is virtually axiomatic that breaking down a given consumer behavior pattern into its constituent parts, attitudes, perceptions, and intent to

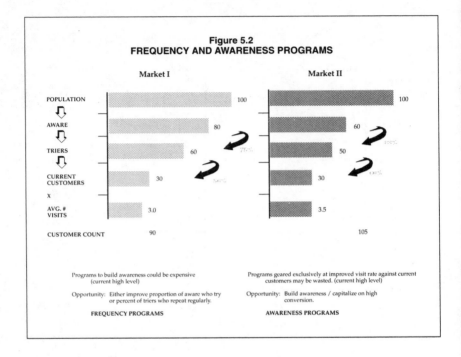

Figure 5.2
FREQUENCY AND AWARENESS PROGRAMS

revisit reveals the most direct way of altering that behavior as desired. It follows that by focusing effort as research indicates, you can exploit the beliefs and impressions—positive and negative—most widely held by your customers. You can also identify areas needing improvement and gaps either across market types or against competition. You will be better able to set standards for operations and concept implementation and to evaluate programs against those standards.

To be more specific about the substance of consumer tracking research, let's examine what kind of things responding consumers are actually asked. "Attribute ratings," for example, are key components that allow researchers to measure and track attitude. To obtain these ratings, interviewers ask consumers to use a 1 to 10 point scale to rate restaurants they've tried on such attributes and perceptions as:

- Value for the money
- Quality of the food
- Freshness of ingredients
- Prompt, friendly service
- Cleanliness

- Variety of the menu
- Convenience of location
- Overall impression

In addition, consumers are asked whether they intend to revisit the restaurant within a specific time period (usually a month) and how often (frequently, once in a while, may or may not, never). During research, the negative responses "may or may not" and "never" are probed with special care to uncover underlying reasons for indifference or definite dissatisfaction. Analysis of these ratings, and of virtually all data gathered, will be done on these bases:

- Absolute terms (levels) for you and competitors
- Relative terms comparing/contrasting you with competitors
- Trended to illuminate the reasons behind behavioral changes

In the initial tracking wave, comparisons of attribute scores of the client's buyer groups (heavy and light users; current customers and triers/rejectors; aware nontriers) are used to help identify those attributes that best "discriminate" among the varying levels of loyalty and usage.

As you undoubtedly realize, these studies are far too intricate to be described fully here. For further illustration and elaboration of the type of useful data that can be generated, assume a hypothetical chain called XYZ. The objectives of XYZ's study might be stated like this:

Interviewing waves will be conducted semi-annually to track awareness, trial, and usage of XYZ and competition across XYZ's system; revisit intentions; attribute ratings for XYZ among various user groups compared to ratings for competitor A; demographics of XYZ's user groups.

Because the study is flexible, a subsequent interviewing wave might include expanded and still more specific objectives:

Investigate past-month non-users of the category in terms of awareness and trial for XYZ; attitudes toward the category; reasons for not trying/visiting XYZ more often; demographic differences in category users; usage of other fast food restaurants.

Compare trends in trade areas where the XYZ Super Special was introduced to areas where it was not.

The results of the tracking study are presented in the form of conclusions and implications drawn from those conclusions. Examples of four sets of conclusions and implications from the hypothetical chain, XYZ, will demonstrate the importance, potential, and range of the tracking study.

Set A Conclusions. Usage of the category among 16 to 65-year-olds in XYZ's trade area has increased significantly. This increase reflects both a larger base of category users and faster visit frequency. XYZ drove category growth with significant share increase to 22 percent over the previous comparable period, when it was 15 percent. The increase was due to higher penetration and average visit frequency. Now, 20 percent of *all* category users have visited XYZ in the past month versus only 13 percent in the previous period. As an entity, XYZ commands a higher visit share than any other direct competitor and dominates its own segment, which is the most popular of the category groupings.

Implication. As the clear category leader, efforts to fuel category expansion should continue to pay dividends.

Set B Conclusions. Within its trade areas, XYZ commands a larger share than all other direct competitors combined. Competition comes from beyond this narrowly defined competitive set. Hamburger fast food restaurants pose the greatest threat to the XYZ shop category, with 32 percent of the fast food visits among the 16 to 65-year-old population in XYZ's trading areas, with the XYZ category taking 17 percent.

Implication. As the category leader, XYZ must compete primarily with hamburger fast food outlets. Benefits that come to mind with these outlets (i.e., fun food, easy to locate and use) need to be understood so that XYZ may capitalize, in advertising and operations, on its similarities with the hamburger units as well as on its uniqueness.

Set C Conclusions. Overall, 41 percent of 16 to 65-year-olds haven't visited the XYZ category in the past month and so are characterized as category nonusers. These people visit fast food restaurants only half as often as category users. Demographically, they differ greatly from regular category users. They are likely to be older (45+), out of the labor force, and with low income. Still, awareness of XYZ is high and almost half of noncategory users have tried XYZ, but frequency is very low. Thirty-seven percent don't think to visit the XYZ category. Thirty-five percent prefer items not offered at the XYZ category.

Implication. Potential among this group is very limited. While some of their attitudes are similar to triers/rejectors, the payout here is certainly lower. They do not fit XYZ's current demographic targets and do not justify adjusting those targets.

Set D Conclusions. Consumers surveyed about XYZ's new Consumate Club sandwich at test locations have fairly weak perceptions of the Consumate Club in terms of awareness, trial, order intent, and price. Seventeen percent were aware of the product. Of those aware, over half said they "probably/definitely will not" order the Consumate Club and only 16 percent will order it. This low order intent reflects apparent lack of consumer information on the sandwich ingredients. Only 18 percent knew of the Consumate Club's basic ingredient. Those aware of the sandwich expressed uncertainty on its price.

Implication. The greatest barrier to consumer trial of the Consumate Club is knowledge. Fast food users avoid the unfamiliar. Further consumer product testing is indicated prior to increased promotion, in order to evaluate consumer satisfaction with the product.

These example sets illustrate the range and potential inherent in the consumer tracking study. A chain commissioning such a study could expect to multiply its impact many times over, with almost limitless possibilities for information critical to strategic planning and market positioning.

Typically, it is suggested that awareness/trial/repeat usage studies be conducted once or twice a year. The semiannual approach is particularly recommended for chains with a record of marketing sophistication. Studies should take place during relatively "average" seasons. It is important that study timing be coordinated to allow for incorporation of results into normal planning cycles.

The scope of the studies also depends on the degree to which a subject foodservice organization makes menu, ad content and spending, and service features decisions on a systemwide basis. If this is accepted procedure in an organization, a controlled number of consumer interviews should be held in each area where the chain has "minimum unit penetration."

To complement a systemwide analysis or as separate research, studies are focused on local or regional markets that represent varying situations such as advertised versus nonadvertised, large units versus small units, intense competition versus limited competition, corporate units versus franchised units.

Actual sample size is determined on a client-by-client basis, with the experience of the research specialists playing the key role in this judgment.

Consistency in administering the studies is critical to result reliability, so all interviews are conducted by trained professionals at a centralized facility. Calls are made during evening or weekend hours to ensure that employed members of the population are represented. Male and female respondents should be equally represented, the appropriate age group questioned, and usage criteria met uniformly.

Following each wave of interviewing, a fully detailed written analysis of all data should be provided by the firm conducting the study within a time period that allows proper interpretation while fitting planning cycle needs. Four weeks is generally an adequate interval between wave completion and the presentation of results. You should also require as part of the research package an executive summary that highlights and concisely discusses major findings, conclusions, implications, and recommendations. Clear charts should support the text of the report.

In the interest of making the most of the study, personal presentations and work sessions should be held that involve all interested parties, including the foodservice firm's upper management, the research specialists, and others on a need-to-know basis.

CHAPTER HIGHLIGHTS AND REVIEW

1) Is your broader-based consumer research effort conducted at key intervals during the year, and is it scheduled to give you continuous trend data?

2) Are you measuring your concept's consumer awareness, trial, and usage levels, and have these key indicators improved over time? What have you done with your concept and advertising programs to influence these indicators?

3) Since the broader-based consumer study addresses the market's perceptions of your business in absolute and competitively relative terms, have you noticed a positive change in your attribute ratings?

4) Are these study results regularly shared within your organization so your colleagues can assist in their interpretation?

5) Have you discarded the posture that you know the results of these studies beforehand, and, therefore do not give them sufficient credence and importance?

Chapter Six

Know Thyself . . . and How!

The key question in this chapter is whether you're getting full mileage from all the sales data and other business records that your foodservice company keeps as a matter of course.

It's not enough to collect data and maintain records. It's not enough to look, say, at topline sales statistics and try to base solid marketing decisions on them. It's not even enough to dig into the topline lode, extract a few isolated marketing nuggets, and think how sophisticated the analysis might be.

To succeed in foodservice, you've got to consistently make the most of the information you should already be collecting regularly, by transforming it into other kinds of specific information, by comparing new ways, by looking at one set of information, by monitoring data meaningfully over time. This chapter presents the procedures proven indispensable to turning mere numbers into marketing magic.

This subject is one of the most difficult to communicate, and not because it is complex. On the contrary, it is simple. Perhaps the difficulty lies in the fact that foodservice providers feel very comfortable and familiar in dealing with meal periods. So, they assume that they already know everything they need to know.

The basepoint of foodservice is the meal period. The foodservice week comprises six distinct dining segments:

- Weekday breakfast (*Monday–Friday*)
- Weekday lunch (*Monday–Friday*)
- Weekday dinner (*Monday–Thursday*)
- Weekend breakfast (*Saturday–Sunday*)

- Weekend lunch (*Saturday–Sunday*)
- Weekend dinner (*Friday–Sunday*)

Key meal periods are distinguished in terms of usage times and by the characteristics of those usage times. So, while weekday breakfast and lunch periods are recorded on Monday through Friday, weekday dinner is recorded on Monday through Thursday. Weekend breakfast and lunch are tracked on Saturday and Sunday, while weekend dinner goes Friday through Sunday. In effect, this results in a three-day weekend and a four-day week for dinner. (There may be other, specialized segments, such as nightclub or late night servings.)

To elaborate on this a bit further consider that, for most concepts, weekday breakfast and lunch are workday meal periods. So any advertising or promotion geared to those periods would be based on the appeal of speed and value. On the weekends, customers for the same periods generally are looking for relaxation, different food quantities, value, and ambience. Further, people who eat at a restaurant at different times usually come from different places. The weekday breakfast and lunch customers probably work in the area, while the weekend customers generally live in the area or are drawn by shopping or other attractions. Weekday dinners, from Monday through Thursday, are usually served to residents, businesspeople, and visitors. Weekend diners tend to be more casual and relaxed and more likely to arrive in family groups, possibly from greater distances and with more time to spend.

So, there is segmentation not only according to meal period, but according to dining experience, mind-set, and geographic distribution. Because different ways of promoting business might apply to each of these segments, you can choose those that are most apt to attract and keep customers—and you will see that by targeting you get more return per promotional dollar spent and promotional energy unit exerted.

Start by collecting sales and other data by meal period. Simply roll up the meal period to get daily data, then roll up to get weekly data, and so on to monthly data. The sales week data report (Figure 6.1) shows how you can do this for total sales.

Now record the dollar sales for each meal period in the designated space. Also record the total daily sales figure where indicated near the bottom of the worksheet. Then, select the first meal period and calculate what percentage of the total day's business falls within this period:

Meal period's sales − total daily sales = % day

Figure 6.1
SALES WEEK DATA REPORT

LOCATION _____   FOR WEEK ENDING _____

DATA	Monday	Tuesday	Wednesday	Thursday	Friday	Saturday	Sunday	TOTAL
Total Sales $								
Customers #								
Entrees / Meals #								
Beverages #								
Appetizers #								
Side Items #								
Desserts #								
Breakfast Sales $								
Breakfast Customers #								
Lunch Sales $								
Lunch Customers #								
Dinner Sales $								
Dinner Customers #								
RATIOS								
Total $ per customer								
$ per entree / meal								
Beverages per customer #								
Appetizers per customer #								
Side items per customer #								
Desserts per customer #								
Breakfast $ per customer								
Lunch $ per customer								
Dinner $ per customer								
Daily sales % of total								
Breakfast Sales %								
Lunch Sales %								
Dinner Sales %								

Repeat the process for all meal periods. Next, go on to calculate what percentage of the week's sales fall on each day of the week:

Daily sales $ − week total dollars = % week

Next, total the sales for weekdays (Monday–Friday) and for weekends (Saturday and Sunday). Then calculate which portion of your business falls during the total weekday period and which portion stems from weekend activities:

Weekday total sales − week total sales $ = % week
Weekend total sales − week total sales $ = % week

But, you are going to collect meal period data not only on sales, but also the number of customers, entrees, beverages, desserts, side items, and appetizers. You can adapt the blank form to record these numbers as well.

From these basic data, you can derive any number of potentially useful averages and ratios, including:

- Customer check average in dollars
- Entree average in dollars
- Beverages per customer
- Desserts per customer
- Side items per customer
- Appetizers per customer

Let's focus on the customer check average as a very basic example. Suppose you had a total weekend lunch time sales of $3,000, and you served 500 customers at an average check of $6.00. You cannot target that average for specific increase, a $1 per customer increase, let's say. Moreover, the beverages per customer ratio is .75:1 If you target that at 1:1, and target an increase in the dessert to a customer ratio of 1:10 while promoting increased sales of these items through an incentive-based suggestive selling plan you might reach your sales increase target. Because you know weekend lunch customers are looking for quantity, leisure, and relaxation, your service people could be instructed to use these ideas in their selling approach, which in turn could be supported by appropriate merchandising of beverages and desserts.

The uses of the base data and the ratios that can be derived from them are essential ammunition for the creative imagination of your marketing department.

CHAPTER HIGHLIGHTS AND REVIEW

1) Is your organization attuned to the importance of accurate and timely data on sales, product, and customer satisfaction?
2) Are records available for a three- to four-week period, and are they regularly maintained?
3) Are data provided to you in an easily accessible and usable format? Are they computerized?
4) Are the sales indicators/ratios given proper weight in measuring productivity at various organization levels?
5) Have you employed such ratios in establishing incentive programs to build sales?

Chapter Seven

Your Menu: Your Marketing Plan in Action

Many foodservice managers suffer from PTM, an affliction that could be fatal to their ability to realize full profitability potential. The cause of PTM—Percentage Target Myopia—is a reliance on the restaurant industry's traditional focus on menu pricing based on percentages rather than on dollars and cents—the conventional cost/multiple pricing method. The root problem with this method is that it grew from cost control concerns rather than marketing concerns—a violation of the marketing perspective principle postulated in the opening chapter of this book. Always remember that your menu is a powerful expression of your strategic marketing plan.

Another basic problem associated with the cost/multiple pricing method is that it ignores guest value while confusing profitability with low food cost percentages. *A 40.5 percent food cost figure is not necessarily more profitable than a 44.9 percent figure.* The following menus (A and B), each with the same items, product cost, and total number of guests, but with different item quantities, illustrate this point with average gross profit per guest differing substantially:

MENU A

Menu Item	Number Sold	Food Cost ($)	Revenue
Chicken	1,000	$1,500	$ 4,500
Steak	400	$1,200	$ 2,800
Lobster	300	$1,350	$ 2,700
Total	**1,700**	**$4,050**	**$10,000**

Potential food cost percentage: $4,050/$10,000 = 40.5%

Total gross profit: $10,000 − $4,050 = **$5,950**

Average gross profit per guest: $5,950/1700 = **$3.50**

MENU B

Menu Item	Number Sold	Food Cost ($)	Revenue
Chicken	300	$ 450	$ 1,350
Steak	800	$2,400	$ 5,600
Lobster	600	$2,700	$ 5,400
Total	**1,700**	**$5,550**	**$12,350**

Potential food cost percentage: $5,550/$12,350 = 44.9%

Total gross profit: $12,350 − $5,550 = **$6,800**

Average gross profit per guest: $6,800/1700 = **$4.00**

It's evident that the menu with the lowest food cost percentage is also the least profitable. Of course, myriad other values must be considered in establishing a menu, but you can see the importance of looking beyond—far beyond—food cost percentages.

The gross profit principle of menu pricing is more advantageous than other methods. The menu analysis process (MAP) is based on that principle, which requires a management focus on gross profit dollars and cents generated by each menu item and not on the item's food cost percentage.

THE MAP PROCESS

MAP allows foodservice managers to make better informed decisions about maintaining, adding, deleting, and promoting menu items. MAP offers the following specific benefits:

- MAP offers an analysis of each competing menu item/guest with the goal of satisfying both buyer and seller, optimizing both popularity and profitability.

- MAP calculates the average penny profit each guest contributes to overhead and profit after paying for the cost of the goods. This information provides the basis for future item pricing decisions (i.e., which items to test for increases and decreases and which items to use for price promotions).

- MAP provides a means of comparatively calculating and scoring the effectiveness of a new menu against its predecessors.

- MAP offers a way of evaluating the effectiveness of existing cost controls by providing a potential or targeted cost of goods to compare against the actual cost of goods.

- MAP provides information to help managers improve menu merchandising of competing items through more effective layout and item location.

This book does not walk you step-by-step through the MAP procedure. Instead, it shows you what you can accomplish by screening the results of that process through the filter of the marketing perspective. It assumes that you've finished the procedures and derived a graph similar to that in Figure 7.1. Note that in the upper righthand corner of the sheet, spaces are provided for the name or location of the restaurant outlet, the foodservice category (appetizer, entree, beverage, dessert, etc.), specific meal period, and date. Each quadrant of the graph is designated by a specific menu classification: Big Winners, Steady Winners, Contenders, and Losers. These classifications are derived from the combination of profitability and popularity ratings shown in Table 7.1.

As you can see, the names of the menu item classifications are chosen more for overall convenience than for complete accuracy. In fact, they represent the mix that makes up most menus. Some even have subclassifications. Some of these subgroups will fall fairly close together on the graph.

Let's start with *Steady Winners*. Located in the lower right quadrant of Figure 7.1, they are relatively high in popularity but below average in profitability. As a rule, however, the Steady Winners are the menu's demand generators.

Steady Winners are further divided into three subgroups. Steady Winners A appear in the upper left area of the Steady Winners quadrant. As are often the lowest price menu items, appealing to the price-

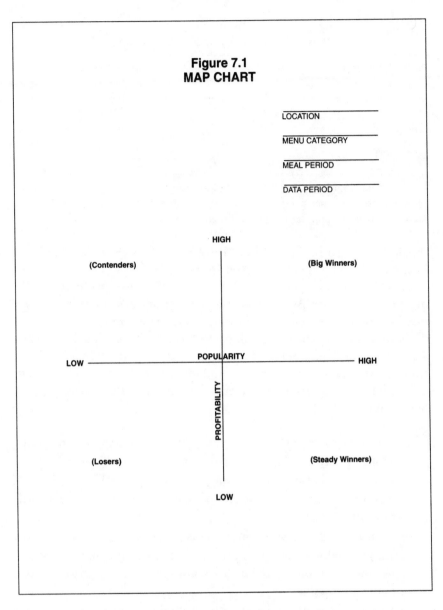

Figure 7.1
MAP CHART

LOCATION

MENU CATEGORY

MEAL PERIOD

DATA PERIOD

sensitive buyer. They broaden the market appeal of the menu and account for much of the total gross profit. As generally should be maintained unchanged for as long as possible. They anchor the lower level of the menu's price points. When this price escalates the other items tend to increase in price as well, risking a drop in demand. As

Table 7.1
Profitability and Popularity Ratings

Profitability Rating	Popularity Rating	Menu Item Classification
High	High	Big Winner
Low	High	Steady Winner
High	Low	Contender
Low	Low	Loser

Note: A menu item's profitability is rated as high or low in relation to category average gross profit per guest. Its popularity rating is determined by whether it is higher or lower in popularity than a category popularity factor.

should be located in areas of low visibility on the menu, that is, placed in the middle of a listing of menu items.

Bs fall into the upper right of the Steady Winners quadrant and are more profitable than As. They are frequently the signature items of your menu—popular and closely tied to the restaurant's image.

Cs are located in the lower half of the Steady Winners quadrant. They account for considerably less of the menu's gross profit, and with a slight shift in either popularity or price could move into another classification.

The following general recommendations apply to the management of Steady Winners:

1) Consider price increases and test price elasticity very carefully.
2) Hold the price as long as possible, if the Steady Winner is one of the menu's lowest price items.
3) Pass on the increase in the cost of goods to the customer. This will not affect gross profit.
4) Increase prices in small increments when testing their elasticity.
5) Employ value-added promotions rather than discounts on Steady Winners, combining them with a low food cost to provide a better value alternative.
6) Calculate the direct labor costs in product preparation to determine labor intensiveness. If the item is highly labor- or skill-intensive, consider price increases or reduce portions subtly.

Big Winners are the items scattered in the upper righthand quadrant of Figure 7.1. They are each category's most popular and most profitable items. They also can be more usefully analyzed by further grouping.

Big Winner As fall in the left side of the upper half of the quadrant and are frequently signature items or house specialties and generate a strong demand. Big Winner As should be carefully monitored for quality and production standards and should be positioned in highly visible spots on the menu.

Big Winner Bs are the menu's most popular and profitable items, found on the right side of the quadrant's upper half. This implies that guests purchasing these items are not as influenced by price as they are by perceived value so that prices may go beyond the normal price range. Items for the "celebration market" are cases in point. These can easily be tested for price elasticity and can effectively be used for price promotions since they contribute more gross profit, even after a discount.

Big Winner Cs are found in the lower half of their quadrant. The higher they are located in the quadrant, the more popular they are and the more important it is to consider changes and test price elasticity. Also, consider eliminating the item, lowering the price to increase demand, or reducing portion sizes to increase profitability.

The following general recommendations apply to Big Winners:

1) Set and maintain rigid production standards and specifications for quality, quantity, and presentation.
2) Place Big Winners in a highly visible location—first on the menu, in a box, or in a special type.
3) Test for price elasticity in small increments.
4) Use these items for promotions during slow periods.
5) Merchandise these items through table tents and suggestive selling.

Contenders are menu items above average in gross profitability, but low in popularity. They are located in the upper left quadrant of Figure 7.1. If there are a number of Contenders on the menu, serious paring should be considered.

Contender As might be derivatives of Big Winners or Steady Winners. In some form, they are already part of the restaurant's inventory. For instance, if a popular item is a 12-ounce cut of prime rib, a Contender A would extend that product to a 15-ounce cut. Contender As require little or no extra effort to produce and should be maintained, but you might lower their prices and achieve an increase in popularity. If the average gross profitability can be maintained in these circumstances, overall menu profitability should increase.

Contender Bs are items that, while not popular, help maintain the restaurant's image. The item might, for instance, be mentioned in the restaurant's name but still be outsold by other items on the menu. These image makers should obviously be kept on the menu.

Contender Cs have no good reason for being on the menu and should be removed.

The following recommendations are appropriate for Contenders:

1) Contenders should be deleted from the menu, particularly if they fall in the lower half of their quadrant, require additional inventory items, have a poor shelf life, cause delays in table turns, have inconsistent quality, require high skill in preparation, or are highly labor-intensive.

2) You can increase the popularity of Contenders simply by reducing the price, adding perceived value through larger portions, or packaging with an add-on item.

3) Reposition the Also-Ran on the menu or change its name.

4) Remove the Also-Ran from the menu.

5) Encourage waitstaff to suggest Also-Rans to customers.

6) Remember that if new menu items should fall into the Also-Ran category, they should be maintained on the menu long enough to test their popularity properly.

Losers, the menu's least popular and least profitable items, are located in the lower left quadrant of Figure 7.1 and with few exceptions should be removed. The losers that should be retained are those that might influence a broader, more desirable market to follow. Children's menu items are an example. Early bird specials might be another way to utilize a loser. Some losers might attract those who could avoid a visit to your restaurant (steak on a seafood menu, for example). Almost any other items in the lower left quadrant are born losers and drop right out of public sight.

MENU DESIGN

The secret to menu design seems to be knowing how the customer's eye travels over the menu on first glance, and what catches the eye, holds attention, and influences the choice of one item over another. Note the word "influence." There are many obstacles to overcome in any attempt to dictate choice, such as personal preference, price, or what the weather might be like. So, menu design may be at best a tenuous science, but it should certainly give you at least a slight edge. And in foodservice those slight edges can add up to success.

The general rule of item placement is that the items listed first in each category (appetizers, entrees, desserts) will sell best. The fact appears to be simply that since we read from top to bottom the first item seen is likely to make a stronger impression, while other items have to fight for attention. Second, we are psychologically conditioned to assume that the item ranked first in a list is Number One, The Winner. The same is true in politics, where top-of-the-ballot placement is considered to be worth more than 8 percent of the vote, all other preferences being equal.

So, what you want to sell most of, place first or set off on the menu. Foodservice providers want to sell most of the items identified by MAP as having the highest gross profit. Also, note that items listed second and last in each category tend to sell better than the remaining items, so you will want to fill these menu spots carefully as well.

Figure 7.2 shows how the consumer's eye ordinarily moves over a menu. On a one-page menu the category of items you wish to sell the most should be placed in the center of the menu. On the two-page menu the printed focus, and prime placement area, is in the center of the second page and at the top of the second page where vision falls twice. On the three-page menu layout, the highest profit items belong in the center of the middle panel and at the top of the righthand panel.

To supplement the edge you can gain in menu placement of high profit items, don't forget that larger type or boxing of items can be extremely effective. Also, make sure that the verbal description of the item is as mouth-watering as possible—with any trendy and tasteful ingredients listed.

Another menu tip from the experts: Physically change your menus daily because today's customer will accept a photocopied or computer-printed menu if it bears the current date and is placed in an attractive holder. The important message it conveys is that your offerings are fresh.

Polls suggest some very interesting things about menu design and the placement of items. For instance, two- and three-page menus are preferred by most diners. The incidence of ordering salad is higher from one-page than from two- or three-page menus. Less popular entrees tend to be chosen more often when the entree list is split into two columns. Faced with a list of six or more items, customers are more likely to order from the top. These poll results emphasize that, although menu design is a tenuous science, it is indeed a science that shouldn't be ignored.

Figure 7.2
MENU PAGE POSITIONING

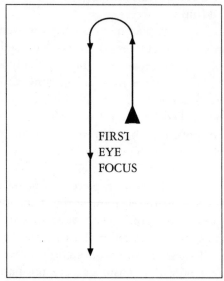

Eye movement across the one-page menu.

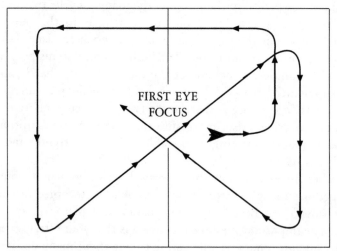

Eye movement across the two-page menu.

And, don't ignore the power of art, either. Make sure your menu presentation is pleasing to the eye. A new look, new logo, new color, or new graphics may well be in order.

The menu board is another method of profitable in-store merchandis-

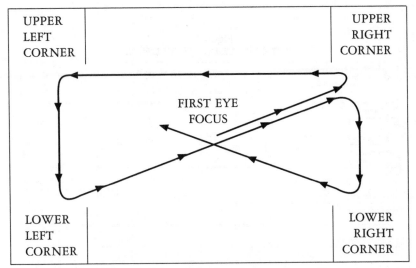

Eye movement across the three-page menu.

ing. Remember, the menu board is the one thing your customers will read. They may not read your newspaper ad or the direct mail piece you sent them; they may not read the message on your reader board or the poster in the front window. But, with few exceptions, every customer who walks in your door reads your menu board. This makes the menu board a valuable selling medium, and it should be considered a selling tool, not a vehicle for displaying attractive photographs/translites.

Some menu boards have space for only one translite, others have space for two, and the newer units have space for three. But, regardless of the number of translites on a menu board, they should be used primarily to sell products. In some cases, a translite may be used to sell a current promotion or campaign, but that's normally a short-term event, and as soon as it's over, product translites should go back up.

There are specific items, offerings, or points of information that are not product-oriented featured in-store from time to time such as specials or promotions, but they can be promoted without using valuable translite space. Use wall or window posters, countercards, or table tents to promote these items.

If it is determined it is important to emphasize something like a Restaurant "Club Card" with a translite, the club card translite should be placed in one of the secondary translite spaces, not in the middle of the menu board, and should be posted only for a limited time and then replaced with a strong product translite.

Figure 7.3
POINT-OF-SALE USAGE GUIDELINES

POINT-OF-SALE	Attract Drive-By Traffic	Attract Walk-By Traffic	Announce Price Special	Announce New Product/ Service	Tell Product/ Service Story	Sell Additional Item	Sell Higher Priced Item
O/S Building Banner (Short/Fast Copy)	A	B	A	A			B
Window Sign (Short/Fast Copy)	A	B	A	A			B
Window Sign (Detailed Copy)		B	A	A	B		B
Reader Board (Short/Fast Copy)	A	B	A	A			B
Wall/Door Poster		B		A	B	A	A
Menu Board Insert Panel				A		A	B
Crew/Employee Button (Short/Fast Copy)				B		A	A
Counter Card				B	B	A	A
Tray Liner				A	A	A	B
Ceiling Mobile				A		A	B
Printed Menu Tip-In				B	B	A	A
Table Promo Piece				A	A	A	A
Customer Service Staff				B	B	A	A
Product Display				B		A	B

A = Primary Application   **B** = Secondary Application

As a general rule, the translite of the product(s) currently being emphasized should be placed in the center (or primary) translite slot. The remaining translite slots, or spaces, should be used to promote popular or high profit items, with a generic or nonproduct translite used only on occasion.

Regardless of how attractive or effective a translite, countercard, or table tent might be, after a certain period of time, the piece loses its impact. The customers have seen it before. It's no longer new, and they don't pay attention to it. The key question is: How long does point-of-sale (POS) material do the job it was designed to do?

In most cases, assuming it's not dirty, torn, or faded, in-store POS material is effective longer than a store manager or franchisee believes. The store manager or the franchisee looks at the POS every day—five, six, even seven days a week. In a short period of time, the POS material almost blends into the background. Depending on visitation frequency, customers will see the POS material only once or twice a month, or once a week, if they are fairly regular customers, not often enough to begin to overlook it within a short period of time. Therefore, in all but the most unusual cases, in-store POS material should be effective for six weeks to two months. Merchandising material used outside the restaurant, such as banners or outward-facing window posters, are usually not effective for quite so long.

People are creatures of habit. They pass by the restaurant day after day on the way to work, on the way home, or going to the mall or shopping center. After they see the banner or window poster a few times, they respond the same way the store manager does—they no longer notice it. So, for any material that is to be viewed from outside the restaurant, a more frequent rotate/replace schedule is needed. Two to three weeks is within reason. The exception to the outside material guideline is the reader board. The message/copy on the reader board should be changed at least weekly.

Use menu board translites primarily to sell the product, to encourage trial usage, to sell side items, to increase check average, or to emphasize a featured product or promotion. The following list of POS usage guidelines should be helpful (see also Figure 7.3):

- Use translites sparingly for generic or nonproduct promotion.
- Rotate/replace translites routinely every six to eight weeks.
- Use merchandising/POS materials other than translites to support nonproduct items.
- Replace outside materials more often than inside materials.

CHAPTER HIGHLIGHTS AND REVIEW

1) Do you have a system for examining and evaluating trend activity of your product line? Is it used regularly?

2) When developing or changing your menu items or prices, do you focus on an overall percentage gross profit or do you place primary emphasis on gross profit dollars?

3) Do you have a strategy that increases profits from your "Steady Winners" group of items?

4) Are you paying special operational attention to your "Big Winners" since they carry the bulk of the business? Also, are you promoting these items—or neglecting them because they're already popular?

5) The "Contenders" require a special plan of attack: Improve them or replace them. Are these items being addressed accordingly?

6) Will the "Losers" be on your menu next month? Or will you turn them into winners?

7) Have you experimented with menu design to promote sales of high profit offerings?

8) Do you use menu boards as the powerful product selling tool they are?

Chapter Eight

Know Thy Enemy or Be Dead in the Water

Knowing your competition is just as important as knowing your customer.

The truth is that in foodservice, as in any consumer-oriented business, competition is the enemy, a hostile force that will not only prevent you from succeeding, but that literally threatens your very business existence.

And, in case you think you're safe, consider what has been happening in banking, merchandising, air travel, and foodservice. Familiar names are disappearing because competition was considered something the other guy engaged in.

You can't beat the competition without getting a first-hand, closeup idea of what you're fighting. Just as incomplete or inaccurate intelligence reporting will affect the outcomes of battles or even wars, so your knowledge of your customers' other restaurant options will determine your success or failure.

But you can't rely on random intelligence reports. You have to be sure that your information-gathering efforts give you the facts that you really need, facts you can act on.

An example of how information can influence the outcome of a competitive business struggle is the classic confrontation between McDonald's and Kentucky Fried Chicken in the early 1970s. McDonald's was deadly serious about moving into the fried chicken market, with the idea of building weekend and evening business around this family-oriented product.

McDonald's chose two test markets, refitted their stores, and equipped them to do a thorough job with fried chicken. They went through a complete product development process and got set to roll out heavy media artillery in the test areas. KFC, however, was alert and paying careful attention to potential incursions. They learned about McDonald's planned testing activity and heavy media schedule and decided to go head-to-head in a media battle to stave off the competition. KFC relied heavily on market observation and data gathering. The upshot was that they prevented a formidable enemy from entering territory that they had staked out for themselves. The conflict had enduring implications for both companies and underscores the real threats posed by competition and how those threats can be warded off through knowledge of your competition— knowledge gained through an established intelligence network respected within your company.

The competitive activity record in Figure 8.1 illustrates the type and extent of the information you should gather. You will see that maintaining this record requires alertness, observation, and, quite possibly, some discreet investigation or questioning. Your advertising agency should give you a great deal of help in this information gathering.

Figure 8.1
COMPETITIVE ACTIVITY RECORD

Location _____

COMPETITOR	DATE	MARKETING ACTIVITY	COMMENTS
Name/Location	Activity Start/Stop	Type/Offer	Reason for Success/ Lack of Success

A good deal of marketing information can be gleaned by paying extra attention to some very commonplace sources: newspaper, magazine, and television advertising as well as the direct mail that comes into your home or office. Networking throughout the industry and casual conversations with colleagues from other firms and geographic areas can be very rewarding if you ask some not so casual questions. And it remains fundamental to visit competitive outlets frequently. In fact, it goes without saying that the search for competitive data should be constant and that the competitive records you keep should be updated regularly.

A competitive activity record will give you a picture of how competitive outlets stack up against your own units. Your restaurant is objectively rated first by characteristic on a scale ranging from excellent to poor. Then, the idea is to look as objectively as possible at each characteristic/attribute for the competitive units and to rate it against the same attribute for your restaurant. So, restaurant "A" might be much better than yours in service speed and restaurant "B" might be much worse. After you rate all the restaurants, you should estimate "average" overall ratings. You will later use these to identify marketing opportunities and to construct your positioning statement.

It is important to identify your real competition. For instance, pizza sellers should place themselves in the same category as other pizza restaurants. Other pizza sellers, *not* burger sellers, are their main competition. Clearly, the pizza and burger firms do compete for the total meal dollar, but the real battleground is demarcated by main product offering.

Obviously, to fill out the competitive evaluation form with any degree of accuracy means having to "shop" the competition often enough to stay current with changes in concept, menu, decor, and so on. Visits should take place regularly, several times a year, to ensure timeliness. The competition survey worksheet presented in Figure 8.2 will aid you in gathering information needed for the competitive evaluation form as well as supplemental observations and data.

Figure 8.2
COMPETITION SURVEY WORKSHEET

Market _____

Location _____

Here are the businesses that compete for my customers:

COMPETITOR	DISTANCE TO MY LOCATION	HOW IT COMPETES WITH MY LOCATION

CHAPTER HIGHLIGHTS AND REVIEW

1) Have you accurately identified those competitors who are seeking to attract your customer base? Are you aware of their strengths and weaknesses?

2) How do you stack up against those primary competitors? Have you developed plans to exploit their weaknesses and to optimize your relative strengths?

3) Is your system for tracking and recording competitive marketing activity functioning smoothly? Are you prepared to respond directly and quickly?

4) Is your entire organization competitively oriented, understanding that "they" are the enemy and that you're fighting a foodservice war in the trenches?

Chapter Nine

Don't Discard the Past —It Could Be Your Future

There is one recurring characteristic of American business that is troubling, perhaps because it seems to be particularly prevalent among corporate and agency practitioners of the foodservice marketing specialty. That characteristic is a tendency to overlook adequate evaluation and recording of what worked and what didn't work in previous sales promotion efforts. Energy and cash are poured indiscriminately into the development and communication of these efforts, driven by a frenetic desire to be ever more creative and to look bright and alert in front of the boss and the client.

Does this scenario sound familiar? Hypothetical project "A" has been in place for a fair period of time. Its results are not reaching stated objectives. What to do? Ninety-nine percent of the time, people tend to throw the project out completely along with all that time and expense. And, it's on to the next thing—naturally something all new.

Such behavior is like buying a car and junking it the first time the engine coughs a bit. It takes much less time to bring the car to the dealer or a service station, have some adjustments made, and be out on the road again than to shop for and finance a new vehicle. So, why not check out the promotional project, see what's wrong, tune it up a bit, and try again? You'll be surprised at how often this works and gratified at the time and money you'll save.

The same "junk it" reaction seems to occur even when a promotion is successful. You'll hear people say, "That promotion we had last year (or the year before) was terrific. It built traffic and sales the way we had hoped." Then you ask why they've taken off a winner and the answer is "Oh, I guess we just thought it was time for something new."

Proven winners, again with some readjustment, can continue to pay off. In fact, you can often improve on them and increase immeasurably the value of the dollars that went into the original effort. That frees up dollars either for the profit line or to go toward the next effort—where it is really needed and will be appreciated in the long term.

You should maintain a record of each promotion that you implement, a record that faces up to shortfalls as well as to successes. Figures 9.1 and 9.2 should be completed for each activity.

What promotion is a success? What promotion is a failure? What promotion might look like a success on paper, but is really a washout because the operational impact is disruptive or because the promotion drew crowds that were too large to serve quickly and alienated customers—customers who will have to be won back?

A major chain once ran a marketwide "buy one, get one free" promotion to combat a soft sales situation. It was scheduled for a summer holiday weekend, which was likely to be busy anyway, and was heavily supported by television and newspaper advertising.

When the first returns were in, things looked good. Sales were up, traffic was up. But profits were nonexistent. The whole exercise was virtually futile as far as the bottom line was concerned.

And then, more really bad news started to come in from the unit managers in the form of some loud complaints. Underlying those sales traffic increases were some real operational crunches. Crowds lined up and waiting, and waiting, and waiting. A scramble to bring in more staff. Product compromised by rushing. The whole experience tarnished by poor service. Lasting negative effects among customers and staff.

A painful memory, but one to learn from. If there had been regular communication between the managers and the marketing group, they would have had a chance to warn about the possibilities of operations programs.

But, beyond that chance, think of how probable it is that this kind of problem is frequently buried. The managers don't wish to make waves; the marketing staff is pleased with the surface figures so nobody says anything. But the organization is damaged, perhaps badly.

A regular system of communications between line management and marketing staff is a necessity. Before a promotion gains unstoppable momentum, seek advice from the men and women who are on the customer contact/operations firing line. And, when the promotion is over,

Figure 9.1
MARKETING PROMOTION HISTORY

PROJECT / ACTIVITY _____

EFFECTIVE DATES _____

OBJECTIVE _____

DESCRIPTION _____
_____
_____
_____

MEDIA _____

COSTS _____
_____

RESULTS _____
_____
_____
_____

ASSESSMENT / SUGGESTIONS _____
_____
_____
_____

Figure 9.2
PROMOTION HISTORY

Market _____

Location _____

PROMOTION PROGRAM DESCRIPTION	DATE	RESULTS

solicit their opinions for true evaluation of its effect and for a firmer basis for future promotional activities.

CHAPTER HIGHLIGHTS AND REVIEW

1) Are you continually evaluating each and every marketing program you've implemented? Is each activity's objective used as the prime evaluation criterion?

2) When is the last time you took an apparent sales-building failure, tweaked it a bit, and turned it into a winner, recognizing that it was simply the media approach, the offer, or the validity period that went sour?

3) How about your winners? Have they been used again, maybe with a different dressing?

4) Does your current marketing plan comprise strictly "new" ideas, or does it include past activities that paid off or perhaps need modification?

Chapter Ten

Flying the Flag on the Fourth of July and Turning Green on March 17

State fairs and county fairs—flying flags, gubernatorial visits, a sense of community, family, patriotism—are an American tradition, particularly in the Midwest. In western states these occasions might be stampedes, rodeos, or pioneer days, but are basically the same as marathons, flower festivals, centennial or other anniversary celebrations, car shows or races, blue grass or classical music gatherings, scouting jamborees, or ethnic celebrations like Columbus Day and St. Patrick's Day.

And as the circumstances are similar so are the opportunities for foodservice companies to participate, not only as vendors but also as community-minded corporate citizens planning and contributing ideas, and providing know-how and sponsorship of the event.

Along with civic reasons there are certainly overriding business reasons for profit-oriented companies to become visible and effective in festivals and celebrations.

The foodservice company needs to recognize that market-level events take people out of their normal restaurant visiting habits. They attract people in family and group clusters to a specific area. While normal retail business can suffer because the customers are elsewhere, the event itself presents sales opportunities. Some companies, for example, maintain mobile serving units to cover fairly widespread major events. They also

Figure 10.1
COMMUNITY ACTIVITIES AND EVENTS

List key activities or events below and assign them a letter code priority of A, B, C, or D, with A being the highest priority.

Activity / Event	Date / Time Frame	Priority (A to D)

make the units available on a priority basis for local celebrations, gaining still more impact for the cost of the unit.

The distribution of promotional literature at and around the event site and running tie-in promotions and discounts supported by the media can also boost sales. Although its focus was a professional sports event, McDonald's exploitation of the rivalry between the Chicago Bears and the Philadelphia Eagles and their coaches when the teams met in 1989 is a case in point. Intense community feeling was tapped. Discounts on different products depending which team won were given prominent publicity, which supplemented paid advertising in the large urban/suburban markets involved.

It may also be possible to stage a companion event to a market-level celebration, such as a 10-k race identified with a state or county fair. The race could raise funds for a charity, providing high visibility to your company and creating another opportunity to sell to the attending crowd.

Beyond the immediate sales opportunities provided by public events and celebrations, and probably even more important, are the long-term gains to be realized in terms of wider awareness of your outlets and a generally more positive image for your company as concerned and active in the community.

But, to successfully take advantage of these situations, you must plan. To plan properly you need timely information, and you get that by looking for it. Membership in state chambers of commerce or tourism organizations is a good way to receive notice of events well in advance, along with a list of contacts who can help you position yourself as a major event participant.

You should see how these major events relate to your various outlets, and then provide reminder, stimulus, and support to local efforts. The chart in Figure 10.1 will facilitate keeping track of coming events and prioritizing them.

CHAPTER HIGHLIGHTS AND REVIEW

1) Is someone in your marketing group keeping an eye peeled for exploitable events? Do you have programs in place to get involved quickly and productively in community happenings?

2) Are you prepared to take your product physically to the market if the event dictates this strategy?

3) What were you doing last year when the fair was in town or a major festival took place? Were you wringing your hands or being hands-on—coming up empty-handed while your competition rang up sales or getting a piece of the business such events offer to you?

Chapter Eleven

Demographics: Making the Numbers Turn into Dollars

The final two steps in the data collection phase of the marketing planning process are closely related. They both focus on the individual market areas in which your restaurant operates and they are both designed to provide a broad understanding of those areas. Taken together, they help define the contexts and conditions in which your restaurant does business and earns profits.

It is surprising how many foodservice marketing professionals don't avail themselves of this type of information. If you do use it, you've got the edge over your competition if they don't. The other side of that coin, of course, is obvious.

First, it is important to understand the dynamics of the economy of your market area. This necessitates an accurate reading of the market area's economic strength or weakness, its growth or decline, as measured by statistics or such economic indicators as new housing starts and retail sales.

This information is not as arcane as it might seem at first glance, but it might require some initial investigation. One place to start could be the business pages of any good regional newspaper, which should carry such information as a matter of course. Another starting point would be the state chamber of commerce. If the chamber staff can't directly supply the specific data you need, they should certainly be able to direct you to reliable sources, probably within the state government. You could start with the public information officers of the appropriate government agencies. Depending on the particular circumstances, it may be more practical to follow similar procedures on a more local level (county, city, or township). In the case of retail sales, for instance, you can look at the records of the agency responsible for the collection of the sales tax. Likewise, you can get information on housing starts from municipal or county building departments, which issue construction permits. Realtors' associations might also provide useful housing start or home purchase activity information.

What you are looking for are trends, comparing current year statistics with those of previous years. You might find, for instance, that housing starts in a given area have been declining over that period, a possible indication of economic decline—or it may mean that the area is fully developed.

To further clarify this type of data and its implications, you may want to examine it in light of other data. If both housing starts and retail sales are trending down, it may be a very poor area for business and traffic growth. If retail sales are up and steady while housing is down, it may indicate that there is simply no more land to build new homes on.

There are commercial services that provide current and projected information by zip code, and these sources can give you a reading on such statistics as projected annual growth rates in regard to the number of households in a given area as well as employment. These commercial services are also a good source for the second area of essential market data: demographics.

Demographics is a term that covers a wide range of information. You can, for instance, learn the population of the area served by each of your units. You can also isolate the percentage of the population of a zip code area that falls into a particular age category. You might find, for instance, that there is a large teenage group in the area, which could supply you with a more profitable promotion target. You can also find past trend data on household income as well as income projections. The services can provide you with an index indicating what people in the area are likely to spend their money on, including dining away from home. Again, you can also identify demographic trends, such as declining population or a growing percentage of seniors in the population.

Important information relating to your restaurant's business and prospects can be drawn from these economic and demographic indicators. The word "indicators" is important. You shouldn't play economist or sociologist with this information. But it can point the way to some very useful details about your business, sometimes by revealing the hidden and sometimes by confirming the obvious by putting information in a slightly different light.

Figure 11.1
MARKET DATA

My Locations/Markets

Date _____

							Total
Number of My Locations							
Number of My Competitors							
Population (000)							
Population/Restaurants Ratio							
Median Income (000)							
Number of Households							
Percentage of Unemployed							
Percentage of White Collar							
Per Capita Income							
Dining Out Index							
Median Age							
My Sales ($000)							

Market Indices - - (100 is Average)

My Locations/Markets

							Total
Population/Restaurant Ratio							
Median Household Income Per Household							
Percentage of Unemployed							
Percentage of White Collar							
Per Capita Income							
Dining Out Index							
My Sales ($000)							

One study, for example, calculated the average population served by a unit of a specific type of restaurant (e.g., pizza) in a given market. That average figured out to be 1:6,500—one pizza restaurant to 6,500 people. Each of the unit's ratios was compared to that average. There was a positive correlation between the population and the sales: the larger the population, the better the sales and vice versa.

Obvious, right? But looked at in this new perspective, it became clear that one low-performing unit really couldn't be expected to improve significantly—the business simply wasn't there and a closing decision, after a last-stand campaign, was indicated. Conversely, the population statistics of another unit, coupled with income data, suggested that this unit could be doing better and a targeted marketing strategy was implemented.

Your staff research or statistical department or specialist, armed with economic and demographic information, should look for ratios of this kind that can be used in making or tempering marketing decisions. You will find that the time and effort invested can yield very high returns when it comes to adding up profitability. The chart in Figure 11.1 will help you to focus on this information. A great resource for support in this area is National Decision Systems, 539 Encinitas Blvd., Encinitas, CA 92024, Phone 619-942-7000.

CHAPTER HIGHLIGHTS AND REVIEW

1) When was the last time your organization looked at the demographic data used to support the location decision for each outlet in your chain?

2) How about checking the locations against today's data? Have they changed? Have you changed your concept or promotional approach in response to these changes?

3) Is your market intelligence network wired into available free demographic data sources? For each location? For each market?

4) Are you applying demographic/competitive ratios to assess prospective sales volume levels by location? By market?

Chapter Twelve

Positioning: Thinking in Reverse to Get into High Gear

The finishing touches needed to round out your marketing plan are your firm's positioning statement and brand personality.

DEVELOPING A POSITIONING STATEMENT

What is a "positioning" statement? To answer that question, you need to put your mind in reverse. True positioning is not what most people think it is. It is the positioning statement, distributed to and understood by your total organization, which creates a thrust and direction for your outlets and helps direct day-to-day operations by providing a base for decision making. A positioning statement is the way in which you inscribe yourself in the minds of others.

Positioning starts with a product—a piece of merchandise, a service, a dining experience, or a person. But positioning is not what you do to a product; positioning is *what you do to the mind of the prospect.* The basic approach to positioning is not to create something new and different but to manipulate what is already in the mind. To develop an effective positioning statement, you must integrate what you are, and what you are capable of doing, with the needs of your market segment.

Some classic examples of positioning can be found in the arena of product marketing. In the soft drink industry, Coca-Cola is positioned in the mind of the consumer as "The Real Thing" and "Coke Is It." Coke was the first cola and has indelibly imprinted the image of Coke as *the* cola in the mind of the consumer. Pepsi, on the other hand, has positioned itself as new and hip—"The Choice of the New Generation." Cigarette companies do a terrific job of positioning their brands. In the mind of the consumer, Marlboro is positioned as a man's cigarette, while Virginia Slims is considered to be a cigarette for women.

Again, positioning requires thinking in reverse. Instead of starting with yourself, you start with the mind of the prospective customer. Ask yourself what your restaurant owns in the mind of the consumer.

The development of an effective positioning statement begins with the determination of the position you already own in the mind of the consumer and the needs of the marketplace. Consumer research is the most definitive method of gathering these data, but it is not always economically feasible for an individual outlet. Failing that, management and staff perceptions can help you answer two key questions: Who buys my product? How do I satisfy their needs?

You must first determine who your customer is. Your customer profiles will vary by meal period, but a simple walk through your outlets during each meal period, looking at the customers rather than at the operations, will provide a base on which you can build a customer profile.

Look at the percentage of visitors versus area residents and workers who patronize your units. Are you getting your fair share of local business? If not, perhaps the position you own in the local marketplace is simply not consistent with the market's needs. Do your customers come in by themselves? In parties of two, three, or four? Your guest checks will indicate the typical party size during each meal period. Your staff can be of great assistance in fine-tuning your customer profile— they have the most direct contact with the customers and can provide details (e.g., age range) which are not otherwise readily available.

Use your findings in these areas to develop a profile of *who buys your product.* Once you have defined your customers, *you must determine how you satisfy their needs.*

To help facilitate the thought process leading up to the creation of your positioning statement, start by making two lists. First, list the consumer benefits (i.e., food value, a place to socialize) you provide, in absolute terms (without regard to your competition). Next, list the consumer benefits you provide relative to the competition. Now, relist the benefits by priority to the consumer. The results should point out that your priorities may be different than the consumer's. The second list—benefits you provide relative to the competition—will provide the basis of your positioning statement. Finally, you should address the following six questions as the starting point for meaningful discussion on a positioning statement or a repositioning statement:

1) What was the "reason for being" that gave you your initial success?
2) What changes have taken place from your original concept? Were they right? Wrong? Should you take another look?
3) Why do people really come to your place? List, and then relist by priority.
4) Are there any differences "out there" that might change your reason for being?
5) Should you consider any changes? List.
6) Have you drifted from the original reasons? Should you go back?

Just how effective an operation's imagery and positioning concepts are has proved to be the difference between success and failure and between mediocre and phenomenal results. McDonald's, for example, certainly did not invent the hamburger. What McDonald's did do was position the hamburger as a total concept to the new customer living in a new environment, through new, clean, suburban, and convenient facilities. Smarter packaging, fast courteous service, good food served quickly at a good price. McDonald's was not a hamburger. It was a unique package of everything the young, mobile, suburban family was looking for at that time. That same opportunity could have been capitalized on by an already existing hamburger or foodservice chain, had they read the environment and matched their resources to it.

Another classic positioning is that of Wendy's against McDonald's, Burger King, et al. Wendy's positioned their entry into the burger jungle with an adult appeal, carving out a segment of market that was looking for something different and better. Wendy's meat, its product quality, its method of preparation, its building ambience, and its communications program all worked in harmony to capture the attention and the dollars of a market that was not a McDonald's or Burger King customer.

Again, positioning is thinking in reverse. Instead of starting with yourself, you start with the mind of the prospect. Instead of asking what you are, ask what position you own in the mind of the prospect. It is much easier to work with the existing perception in the prospect's mind than to change it. In determining the state of your prospect's mind, don't assume they see you as you want to be seen. What is important is the way you are actually thought of. Do not let big boss egos get in the way of this. You will get the *correct* answer from the marketplace, not the president.

Getting the correct answer to "what position we own" may cost additional dollars in research, but it is an investment, not a wasteful expenditure. It's better to know exactly what you are up against now, than to discover it later when nothing can be done about it.

Look at 7-Up, for example. Their problem was not the prospect's attitude toward a lemon-lime drink, but rather the overwhelming share of mind occupied by the colas. From the 7-Up perspective, "Get me a soda," to too many people meant a Coke or Pepsi. Looking at the big picture helped 7-Up develop its successful un-cola program.

Most products, services, and concepts today are like 7-Up before the un-cola campaign. They have a weak or nonexistent position in the minds of most prospects. What must be done is to find a way into the mind by hooking your product, service, or consent to what is already there.

As a further guide to what your positioning statement should look like, read the following hypothetical statement for the Chapultepec, a quick turnover (less than one hour) dinnerhouse and bar servicing the mass market (takeout is available). The concept emphasizes food and freshness.

CHAPULTEPEC POSITIONING STATEMENT

The restaurant features Mexican, grilled, and contemporary foods served in a Mexican style appropriate for lunch, dinner, and snack occasions.

The bar features great Margaritas, fruit based drinks, wines, Mexican beers, and a standard selection of mixed drinks and domestic/imported beers.

The concept is targeted to adults either with or without children present at the meal occasion. The restaurant and bar work together to bring consumers a fun experience. This benefit is delivered by:

- A wide variety of unique foods, Margaritas, and other drinks that add to the fun because they are attractive, large/impressive, and are perceived as fresh. The food is available in various "spiced" levels and the menu is regionalized to meet the needs of unique markets.

Figure 12.1
POSITIONING STATEMENT WORKSHEET

1. **Customer Profile**—indicate who your customers are by meal period and by weekpart:

Meal Period: _____	Meal Period: _____
Weekday	**Weekday**
Area visitors _____ %	Area visitors _____ %
Local residents _____ %	Local residents _____ %
Average party size _____ %	Average party size _____ %
Age range _____	Age range _____
Gender:	Gender:
Male _____ %	Male _____ %
Female _____ %	Female _____ %
Weekend	**Weekend**
Area visitors _____ %	Area visitors _____ %
Local residents _____ %	Local residents _____ %
Average party size _____ %	Average party size _____ %
Age range _____	Age range _____
Gender:	Gender:
Male _____ %	Male _____ %
Female _____ %	Female _____ %

Positioning Statement Worksheet - Page 2

2.   List the consumer benefits you provide, in absolute terms (without regard to the competition):

_____   _____

_____   _____

_____   _____

_____   _____

3.   List the consumer benefits you provide relative to the competition:

_____   _____

_____   _____

_____   _____

_____   _____

4.   List the benefits by priority to the consumer:

_____   _____

_____   _____

_____   _____

_____   _____

5.   List any other attributes you wish to convey to the consumer:

_____   _____

_____   _____

_____   _____

_____   _____

- Enthusiastic, friendly, and knowledgeable servers who act natural (unstructured) and develop a rapport with guests so they feel comfortable having a good time.

- A bar that emphasizes food and fun and evolves into a more adult/ social environment as the evening progresses—normal happy hour and increasingly higher energy levels (music, promotions) from 9:00 P.M. until close.

- A decor level targeted to each market, which is perceived as southwestern/contemporary and which encourages a fun mood.

- A generally low/moderate pricing level for both lunch and dinner with a few higher-priced items ($9.00 plus).

The elements of the restaurant and bar work together to provide great food and drinks, a fun experience, and a good value for our guests.

Your positioning statement will incorporate all the attributes of your restaurant that you wish to convey to the consumer, from the decor to the type of service and hours of operation.

(A positioning statement worksheet is shown in Figure 12.1. For more insight on positioning, refer to Appendix G, "You Don't Have to Be Number One to Be Number One: The Positioning Pitfall.")

BRAND PERSONALITY

Closely related to positioning is brand personality, that "something" which sets your restaurant apart from all others in the mind of the consumer. Without a clearly defined brand personality, you will not be able to fully realize your position in the marketplace.

The "something" that is brand personality comprises several key elements: what you look like, what you do, and how you work. But what really characterizes brand personality is the psychological bond it creates between you and your customers, the emotional attachments based on fixed perceptions that draw the customer to you.

This description may sound a bit high-flown but it comes down to a basic truth: Brand personality differentiates you from the competition and in many instances can be the crucial element in establishing your competitive uniqueness. It replaces conscious choice as an element in making a purchase.

Let's look again at two tobacco products that have established brand personality. Say Marlboro, and you conjure a picture of a rugged outdoor man with a macho presence. Most of those buying Marlboro identify with this image, automatically, and buy almost by reflex. Then, you have Virginia Slims, clearly and consistently pitched to the feminine market. That image is reinforced by the women's tennis tournaments the company sponsors.

To switch examples, consider Oil of Olay, represented by an ageless, sophisticated, mysterious, and slightly exotic woman. Or, there's Johnson's Baby Powder, which makes people feel good both physically and mentally, emanating confidence, evoking memories of childhood and a special heritage associated with honesty, simplicity, quality, and purity. Dr. Pepper is the brash new kid on the block with an outgoing, fun-loving youthful irreverence that establishes the product as unique and original and gives the consumer a taste of individuality.

To summarize what you should be looking for in developing your restaurant's brand personality:

Character is usually the most important aspect of brand personality. It involves discovering and exploiting the psychological bond that exists between your restaurant and how consumers perceive it, feel about it, and relate to it. To the consumer, you can appear like an old friend, an authority figure, a good-time buddy; your brand personality can be dependable, exotic, refreshing; it can be a luxury, a treat, or a necessity.

Functionality is what you do. All restaurants present food so what do you provide beyond, or in addition, that will set you apart? Is your restaurant fun, good for parties, for meetings?

Physicality is what the restaurant looks like—busy, lived-in, a home-away-from home.

In personifying your business, you create a portrait using the basic categories of age, sex, emotional qualities, intelligence, and sense of humor. You must also build on your customer's sense of familiarity and loyalty.

Following is an example of how one restaurant states its brand personality:

She (the restaurant) is a treasured member of the family who lives nearby. She is amazing to you (the customer) because she has a great time no matter what she's doing, and when you're with her so do you. Her enthusiasm for life is practically infectious. To her, nothing is ordinary, and boring just isn't in her vocabulary. That's why you enjoy spending time with her.

And no matter who you bring to visit her—old friends, new friends, family—everybody likes her. She's lively and full of surprises. So no visit is exactly the same as the last. Yet underneath all of this activity is a warmth that makes you feel welcome and comfortable.

Her house is casual and always bustling. It's not messy but has a lived-in feeling. On your way home from visiting her, you always make a comment about what a good time you had. Even if you were down or tired when you came, the visit is rejuvenating and leaves you feeling more carefree.

Once you've established a clear brand personality, be aware that tampering with it can be hazardous. It is a point of constancy in a volatile marketplace. As long as your target audience remains the same, there should be no reason to change your brand personality. In fact, it is interesting to see how many established companies have recently been returning to ads that call on the nostalgia evoked by their brand personality to reattract and retain long-time customers.

CHAPTER HIGHLIGHTS AND REVIEW

1) Your positioning statement is the way you inscribe your restaurant in the minds of your prospects.
2) Positioning demands answers to two questions: Who buys my product? How do I satisfy the buyers' needs?
3) Your brand personality is that "something" which sets your restaurant apart from all others in the mind of consumers.
4) Brand personality comprises what you look like, what you do, and how you work.
5) Brand personality is a point of constancy in a volatile marketplace.

Chapter Thirteen

What It All Means: Analyzing the Data

The planning phase that separates the top-flight foodservice marketers from the second-tier practitioners, the winners from the also-rans, is analysis of the data. Here is where instinct honed by experience comes into play. Judgment, downright savvy, and smarts are critical qualities when it comes to interpreting the data and drawing from them the pertinent conclusions that are the foundation of your marketing plan's objectives and strategies.

Data collection is the province of support staff. It's how they contribute to the planning process and how they wean themselves from the textbooks and start to learn what foodservice marketing is really all about. Data analysis, however, is the responsibility of the senior marketing executives—the Joe Montanas, Greg Normans, Steffi Grafs, and Jose Cansecos of foodservice marketing. You and your peers are about to take your turn at bat, rush the net, chip for eagle, pass to Jerry Rice.

REPORTING THE RESULTS

All the data that the planning process required have been assembled, the various worksheets have been filled out, and a final report has been prepared and highlighted for your study. Now you can take the reported facts and turn them into useful conclusions for building your marketing objectives and strategies.

It is helpful to understand what conclusions are and are not. Start with sales data for a hypothetical group of foodservice outlets:

Data Highlights	*Conclusions*
Weekend dinner traffic shows little/no growth.	Competition has attracted some weekend dinner customers with its offers.
Competition has focused its marketing on this segment with weekend dinner discount offers.	
Thursday through Saturday represents 60 percent of weekly sales.	Customer purchase patterns are skewed toward late week and the weekend. Media scheduling should reflect this clearly established pattern.

You can see that highlighted sales data were interpreted—not just repeated or restated—to form an implication. The progression here is from facts to conclusions based on those facts, not from reported fact to restated fact. The difference is one of substance not just of degree. The process changes from record keeping to creativity, from science to art. And, notice that at this point, the process stops short of delineating specific objectives.

To further illustrate the distinction between data and conclusion, look at the following:

BEVERAGE SALES

Data	*Conclusion*
The ratio of beverage unit sales to entrees bought is .65:1.	Not all customers buy a beverage with their meal. There is room for improvement in this ratio and for sales and profit increases.

It is critical that you resist the temptation to leap from data to obvious objectives and strategies, omitting the implication step. This leap removes the creative touch and simply leads to doing the same old thing over and over again. If it were that easy, achieving foodservice success would be no challenge. It would require only limited experience; anybody could do it. Success requires a creative spark, focus and concentration, and, quite often, collaboration among experienced marketers. Drawing the right conclusion from the assembled data is what gives you and your peers your day in the sun.

That day, however, could be even sunnier and longer if you pause to rank the weaknesses and strengths you identified according to the following criteria:

Urgency (How serious is the weakness? How outstanding or opportune is the strength?)

Achievability (Can the weakness be attacked or the strength developed through reasonable and economical marketing efforts?)

OBJECTIVES AND STRATEGIES

Even among the most clearheaded the distinctions among objectives, strategies, and tactics remain blurred. This confusion is not only definitional, it is also positional. The head of a corporation makes a strategic statement. Top-rank subordinates develop that strategy into a series of objectives. The second-rank subordinates charged directly with execution refine it into a set of tactics. Each rank refers to all of the stated goals from their own particular perspective, adding to organization confusion.

From the outset you need to recognize that objectives define what needs *to be achieved* while strategies define what needs *to be done* to achieve those objectives. Objectives and strategies, once structured, have to be written in a format that is clear and easily understandable so as to provide guidance and direction (not confusion) to your support staff— in-house personnel or outside suppliers—who are charged with the implementation and development of your marketing activities.

An objective is a detailed statement of purpose. It should be quantifiable, calling for a measurable result and posting a time at which the measurement should occur. An objective is a practical, specific target to be reached within set time limits. Base your objectives on the problems/opportunities you have identified. That list is the "raw material" on which your objectives are set. Be careful not to set your sights too high or too low when defining objectives—your goals must be attainable but challenging. In addition to being meaningful and achievable, your objectives should be measurable. You build in a prime element of measurability when you include a time limit. When that time has elapsed, you will be ready to evaluate the results of your efforts.

Use these guidelines in setting your objectives:

- Be practical.
- Set specific targets.
- Set time limits.
- Assure means for measuring success or failure.

Once your objectives are clearly defined, a plan for achieving them must be formulated. This plan will be the strategy. Keep in mind that the strategy may partially repeat the objective, but it will invariably extend it, *stating a general action to be taken and a customer grouping against which that action will be targeted*—in other words *to whom and what,* but not how. A number of strategies may be implemented for each objective. The strategy planner must choose the strategy that best suits the objective. The planner then adopts certain tactics.

The sequence is illustrated as follows:

Objective:

- Achieve a sales level of plus 4 percent compared to the same months last year for the period April through September (1992 versus 1991).

Strategies:

- Focus on families in immediate residential area to attract new customers.
- Provide stimulus for increasing customer traffic during weekday dinner and evening hours.
- Develop contacts with local schools, then create a school-oriented promotion that will be jointly beneficial.
- Create incentives for trial of food products from existing customer base.

Tactics:

- Place door knob coupons on doors of residential homes and apartments in zip code 34567.
- Offer a "Report Card Incentive" program to area students.
- Distribute special anniversary bounceback coupons to customers for food products on their return visit during the June anniversary time period.

- Offer evening restaurant customers a special admission to a family movie.
- With a minimum purchase during the first two weeks of May, a customer can receive a discount on floral arrangements around Mother's Day.
- With a minimum purchase during the first two weeks of June, a customer receive one free visit to a local fitness center around Father's Day.
- A customer can receive entry blank/coupon at retail locations and redeem it at your restaurant for a special food offer and chance to win a shopping spree at a tie-in local retail business.

CHAPTER HIGHLIGHTS AND REVIEW

1) Are you accessing all the "brains" and sophistication available to you when interpreting your market intelligence? Other departmental executives? Your agency? Your research resource?

2) Do the interpreted conclusions—strengths and weaknesses—clearly lead to a series of objectives and strategies as the foundation of your overall marketing plan?

3) Is each component of the marketing mix defined with its own set of clearly defined objectives and strategies?

4) Are you prepared to fully defend your objectives and strategies to upper management and/or the owners of the business you are charged with managing?

Chapter Fourteen

Marketing Programs: Where the Fun Really Is

An important task in foodservice is to devise the tactics that fulfill and implement the objectives and strategies you've structured. In the context of foodservice marketing, these tactics are called promotional programs.

Such programs are varied by nature, and that variation is limited only by the imagination directed toward their development. But, despite their differences, successful programs have many things in common—most notably, a set structure and consistent follow-through. They also employ the principle of vertical integration and adhere to some basic rules. And they fall into certain definable categories, each of which presents its own combination of potential opportunities and pitfalls.

VERTICAL INTEGRATION

Successful programs almost universally adhere to the principle of vertical integration. Vertical integration is based on the concept that the total marketing function comprises closely related tiers or levels, all of which support the same advertising message. If one tier is ignored, slighted, or improperly executed, the promotional effort will fall short of its maximum potential upward impact on sales. The levels are identified as:

- Broadcast—television or radio (often the best reach buy for the media dollar as well the most easily prepared material) commercial and promotional spots
- Print—newspapers, magazines, direct mail, and fliers
- Local promotions and community involvement

- In-store activities and staff incentive programs

As an example, let's say that you plan a promotion for Halloween. The four tiers would be deployed in this way:

- Television/radio spots featuring Halloween-theme promotion: Emphasize that Halloween will be a fun occasion at your units and promotions will be available.
- Newspaper: Announce the event with a specific invitation for kids to attend.
- Local promotion: Invite neighborhood kids to wear costumes in order to receive a Halloween cookie.
- In-store activities: Display Halloween Point of Sale (POS), and hold a staff costume contest.

Vertical integration allows you to concentrate your advertising budget on one program, multiplying the effect of each dollar spent. The positive impact is even greater when you consider that you are not diluting your message by going off on random promotional tangents. You will find that the "promotion" has been turned into a campaign with heightened potential.

DISCLAIMERS AND DISCLOSURES

The fundamental role of advertising disclaimers and disclosures is often overlooked. They are essential to clarifying offers so that consumers can properly and easily understand them, and they help significantly in controlling the honoring of promotional offers. The following guidelines should be followed in the creation of any program:

Product Size and Specifications. Clearly identify the menu item you are promoting to avoid confusion and possible customer disappointment and confrontation. If the offer is $1.00 off a "Royal Mushroom Burger," say so. Don't say a "Burger" or "Royal Burger" in your promotional material. If you offer a free soft drink, specify the size and type: "12-ounce root beer," not just "soft drink."

Price/Discount. Again, a clear statement of what you are offering, but with the reenforcement of contrasting the "save price" with the "regular price": $1.00 off a "Royal Mushroom Burger," regular price $3.59, $2.59 with coupon.

Where to Find the Offer. In smaller markets, listing your locations will help customers find your restaurant. In larger markets, the statement "offer good at participating XYZ restaurants" should suffice.

Expiration Date. Make sure that the offer's expiration date is explicit and easily readable.

What to Do. Some promotional offers require customers to do something, to bring a coupon, to buy two "Royal Mushroom Burgers," to visit an XYZ restaurant four times within 30 days. These "action" instructions should be spelled out in detail.

Avoid Double Hits. State clearly that the "Offer is not valid in conjunction with any other promotional offer."

Limitations. If you wish to limit the number of promotional items per customer, say how many: "One Royal Mushroom Burger to a Customer."

Time and Day Restrictions. You may be targeting the promotion to increase weekday lunch business, so state the restriction: "Offer good between 11 A.M. and 2 P.M., Monday through Friday."

Remember that each purchase qualification you build into a promotion reduces the opportunity, and possibly the attraction of a customer to visit your restaurant. Include the necessary, omit the extras, and you'll have the building blocks for a creative, attractive ad. (The ad samples in Figure 14.1 underscore the need to stress disclaimers and show how they sometimes add to the pull of the advertisement.)

HOLIDAYS

Traditional holidays offer many opportunities for promotion. First, many of them are already associated with gift giving and shopping so that people are out of their homes and more likely to spend impulsively; moreover, they are in a festive mood and feel like doing something different. Your promotion becomes part of a sweeping campaign waged by retailers and other merchants and service providers.

Some of the more promotable holidays and occasions you should make part of your marketing calendar include:

- New Year's Day
- Valentine's Day
- President's Day

Figure 14.1
SAMPLE ADS

THIS OFFER
EXPIRES
IN TEN DAYS

rts museums, includ
Cooperstown, with its re
auditorium: the Professio
Canton, Ohio: and the ne
Hall of Fame, featuring s
and games. Football fans
issue. Amopco Motor Clu
the NFL's upcoming sea
ure, modern-day explorer
California, a region poss
iderness areas - vet minu

le contrasts. Here, start de
de Cristo
ries-old Indian trail; well-
pre ew buildings; and world
nate. When visiting, don't
miss New Mexico, villages
- so have reinstated the

for Marilyn's look at thi

JOE'S
RESTAURANT

tisher. Editorial correspond
bers requets should be
ture Road. c/o Conde for

66601. 1989. All rights
<axwell Graphics Gro
Second-class postage

year, and to nos mem
$4.50 per year Send
made payable to Adv

GOOD ONLY AT
PARTICIPATING
RESTAURANTS.

rts museums, includ
Cooperstown, with its re
auditorium: the Professio
Canton, Ohio: and the ne
Hall of Fame, featuring s
and games. Football fans
issue. Amopco Motor Clu
the NFL's upcoming sea
ure, modern-day explorer
California, a region poss
iderness areas - vet minu

le contrasts. Here, start de
de Cristo
ries-old Indian trail; well-
pre ew buildings; and world
nate. When visiting, don't
miss New Mexico, villages
- so have reinstated the

for Marilyn's look at thi

JOE'S
RESTAURANT

tisher. Editorial correspond
bers requets should be
ture Road. c/o Conde for

66601. 1989. All rights
<axwell Graphics Gro
Second-class postage

year, and to nos mem
$4.50 per year Send
made payable to Adv

THIS OFFER
IS GOOD ONLY
ON WEEKENDS.

rts museums, includ
Cooperstown, with its re
auditorium: the Professio
Canton, Ohio: and the ne
Hall of Fame, featuring s
and games. Football fans
issue. Amopco Motor Clu
the NFL's upcoming sea
ure, modern-day explorer
California, a region poss
iderness areas - vet minu

le contrasts. Here, start de
de Cristo
ries-old Indian trail; well-
pre ew buildings; and world
nate. When visiting, don't
miss New Mexico, villages
- so have reinstated the

for Marilyn's look at thi

JOE'S
RESTAURANT

tisher. Editorial correspond
bers requets should be
ture Road. c/o Conde for

66601. 1989. All rights
<axwell Graphics Gro
Second-class postage

year, and to nos mem
$4.50 per year Send
made payable to Adv

NOT GOOD
WITH ANY
OTHER OFFER.

rts museums, includ
Cooperstown, with its re
auditorium: the Professio
Canton, Ohio: and the ne
Hall of Fame, featuring s
and games. Football fans
issue. Amopco Motor Clu
the NFL's upcoming sea
ure, modern-day explorer
California, a region poss
iderness areas - vet minu

le contrasts. Here, start de
de Cristo
ries-old Indian trail; well-
pre ew buildings; and world
nate. When visiting, don't
miss New Mexico, villages
- so have reinstated the

for Marilyn's look at thi

JOE'S
RESTAURANT

tisher. Editorial correspond
bers requets should be
ture Road. c/o Conde for

66601. 1989. All rights
<axwell Graphics Gro
Second-class postage

year, and to nos mem
$4.50 per year Send
made payable to Adv

Figure 14.1 (*continued*)

THIS OFFER
IS GOOD ONLY
FOR KIDS.

rts museums, includ
Cooperstown, with its re
auditorium: the Professio
Canton, Ohio: and the ne
Hall of Fame, featuring s
and games. Football fans
issue. Amopco Motor Clu
the NFL's upcoming sea
ure, modern-day explorer
California, a region poss
iderness areas - vet minu

le contrasts. Here, start de
de Cristo
ries-old Indian trail; well-
pre ew buildings; and world
nate. When visiting, don't
miss New Mexico, villages
- so have reinstated the

for Marilyn's look at thi

JOE'S
RESTAURANT

tisher. Editorial correspond
bers requets should be
ture Road. c/o Conde for

66601. 1989. All rights
<axwell Graphics Gro
Second-class postage

year, and to nos mem
$4.50 per year Send
made payable to Adv

BRING THIS
COUPON
TO A
PARTICIPATING
LOCATION.

rts museums, includ
Cooperstown, with its re
auditorium: the Professio
Canton, Ohio: and the ne
Hall of Fame, featuring s
and games. Football fans
issue. Amopco Motor Clu
the NFL's upcoming sea
ure, modern-day explorer
California, a region poss
iderness areas - vet minu

le contrasts. Here, start de
de Cristo
ries-old Indian trail; well-
pre ew buildings; and world
nate. When visiting, don't
miss New Mexico, villages
- so have reinstated the

for Marilyn's look at thi

tisher. Editorial correspond
bers requets should be
ture Road. c/o Conde for

66601. 1989. All rights
<axwell Graphics Gro
Second-class postage

year, and to nos mem
$4.50 per year Send
made payable to Adv

Figure 14.1 (*continued*)

- Mother's Day
- Secretary's Day
- Fourth of July
- Your unit's Grand Opening/Anniversary/New Product Intros
- Local business/shopping promotions such as Sidewalk Sales, Mall Dollar Days
- Special local events: County fairs, marathons, auto races, festivals, etc.
- Father's Day
- Labor Day
- Memorial Day
- Halloween
- Easter
- Christmas
- Hanukkah
- Back-to-School
- Thanksgiving
- Local holidays

There is also the possibility of creating your own holiday. Be aware of community events and happenings. For instance, is a local professional, collegiate, or high school team having a contending or championship season? If so, you've got a natural promotion right at your fingertips.

TYPES OF PROMOTIONS/OFFERS

Promotions fall into general categories, each with its own purpose or purposes and its own attractions, and some with a few cautions to be observed. But, all sales promotions share the same desired result: to give the consuming public an extra incentive to choose your restaurant over your competition.

Promotion offers may be either "open" or "contingent." An "open" offer requires the consumer to do nothing except purchase the offered item. For example, lunch specials, menu price reductions, and no purchase necessary premiums are open offers. The advantage of open offers is that they broaden consumer appeal because people tend to be somewhat lazy and don't want to take the time required to clip a coupon or present a punch card. The downside risk, which is very real, is that the promoter has virtually no control over the redemption rate—which could climb to a very costly level.

Some restaurant operators try to realize the appeal advantage of the open offer—no customer action necessary—while trying to hide the offer at the point of sale. Their intent is to maximize the traffic created by the offer without honoring the offer. They're banking on people forgetting—which they sometimes do. This kind of behavior is unethical and should not be practiced. Give the customer the deal you've offered!

An acceptable tactic, however, is to attempt to trade customers up at the point of sale—building on the offer with natural logical extensions. Let's say your open offer is "Eight pieces of chicken, only $4.99. Regular price $6.99." Your point-of-sale materials could include these tradeup offers:

Eight pieces—$4.99 (regular value $6.99)
Eight pieces with two salads—$6.99
Eight pieces with two salads and six biscuits—$7.99

This approach could be extremely effective with customers who come in for the $4.99 special, because they will perceive extra value.

The "contingent" offer is much the converse of the open variety. The customer is required to take some action to benefit from the offer, whether it be to make a specific purchase (buy a "Royal Mushroom Burger" and get a free 12-ounce root beer) or bring in a coupon and get 50¢ off the price of the burger. And, while the redemption rate is controlled more easily, the consumer appeal is considerably narrowed. Over the long haul, however, the contingent promotion is preferable. Redemption rate and redemption cost control are key factors in the choice.

PRICEOFFS/DISCOUNTS

Priceoffs and discounts are undoubtedly the most frequently employed promotional incentives in the foodservice industry. A typical priceoff structure might be:

50¢ off any sandwich
$1.00 off any two sandwiches
$1.00 off any complete meal
$2.00 off any complete meal

Presenting offers in this fashion enables you to place an exact value on the coupon while broadening the offer's appeal by using the word "any," which makes the priceoff available for all sandwiches/meals. Of course, you may be attempting to build trial of a specific item, in which case you would simply change the offer wording to include that "Royal Mushroom Burger" again.

Discounts are similar to priceoffs, the difference residing in the presentation of the offer:

Royal Mushroom Burger, now $2.59 with coupon—regular price $3.25

Two Royal Mushroom Burgers for $5.18 with coupon—regular normally $6.25

Lunch Special—$3.00 with coupon, normally $4.00

Experience indicates that a 15 to 20 percent price reduction provides sufficient incentive for the consumer to buy. Once again, though, the final choice of the price reduction is yours, subject to competitive and other conditions.

FREE OFFERS

"Free" is one of the most powerful promotion words available. It commands and gets attention, and it usually generates immediate response. Free offers are used when your purpose is to create consumer "trial" or "retrial" of your main or secondary product or of a new product. *Note:* Whenever you make a free offer, always use a coupon to control redemption.

A widely used free offer is "Buy one, get one free," which has broad appeal since most consumers will dine with another individual or, if the offer applies to a sandwich, may well eat two sandwiches. While this is a costly promotion offer, you'll invariably realize a substantial increase in the sales of high profit beverages and side items. But remember that your prime objective is to gain trial, and that the true measurement of the success of a BOGOF offer is an increase in customer count.

Other free or value-added offers might be:

Buy two, get one free

Buy one sandwich, medium fries, and medium soft drink and get second sandwich free

Free dessert with purchase of complete meal

You should not offer a free beverage. A free beverage lacks real consumer appeal; moreover, such an offer is often a detriment to sales totals and profits since most customers purchase a beverage anyway.

PREMIUMS

Although widely used, premiums generally produce results that can best be described as mixed. In selecting a promotional premium, you must be careful to balance cost versus real appeal—a line that is easier to talk about than to walk when you're making the premium decision. Another way of stating this "must" in premium selection is that you have to select a specific target audience and match your premium to the requirements and interests of that audience. And a caution is in order: Don't rely on premiums as the linchpin of your promotional efforts.

If you have an adult audience, you can probably start and stop with "glasses" as a premium—the success of alternatives has been almost nonexistent. The appeal of glasses lies in their basic practicality. Glasses are always used in the home and are frequently broken, so consumers have a continuing need for them. Add to this practicality the entertainment and fun value of glasses—a tie-in to a popular professional sports team usually works well—and you could well have a winner.

From the promoter's vantage point, glasses are affordable, particularly when linked to the purchase of a larger (high profit) size beverage. This leads to another important observation about premiums: They should always be tied to the purchase of a higher profit item such as the large beverage or the more fully garnished meal or sandwich. Remember, too, the promotion should be structured to encourage purchase frequency.

There is another premium category that holds some promise of success—because it can be produced and procured at relatively low cost. This is the printed youth premium, which is flexible because the "kids" audience is particularly susceptible to changing fads and because its application is limited only by your staff's imagination, creativity, and sensitivity to popular trends.

MEAL PACKS

The underlying objective of a meal pack promotion is to build per meal expenditures, measured as a dollar price per basic menu item. These sales promotions featuring complete meals have, for the most part, been effective in meeting their stated goal.

Meal packs consist of adding side items to the basic menu item to create a complete meal for one or more customers. The addition of a drink as part of the pack rounds out the meal and adds profitability. Depending on the size and variety of your menu, the possible meal pack combination is almost endless, depending on what you decide will be most attractive to your customer base. But while deciding what to include in the pack, keep in mind that your pricing of the pack must be meaningful.

The goal of meal pack promotion—to increase per meal expenditure—requires you to focus on an increase in absolute profit. To achieve this, you will need to sacrifice product cost percentage. As an example, if you typically charge $3.50 per basic item and your food and paper costs run 32 percent of the charge, your gross profit will be $2.38. If you increase per meal revenue to $4.50 with a discounted pack offer, your F&P costs could rise to 40 percent, but your gross profit will be $2.70—and you've completed a successful promotion.

PURCHASE FREQUENCY PROMOTIONS

Purchase frequency promotions are intended to encourage your customers to purchase meals at your restaurant at a faster rate than they would normally. Glass promotions fall into this category. But exhibiting another limitation of premium offers, they usually fade in interest over a fairly short period of time, returning the frequency rate to normal. Bounceback coupons are effective in stimulating purchase frequency. Giving the customer a certificate good for a product offer on a return visit works well and may be used to attract customers to another meal period in which sales need to be bolstered. Other frequency builders are "clubs." A breakfast club, for instance, might offer a free breakfast after the purchase of five breakfasts in a month. In addition to controlling the offer, club punch cards should carry clear information on the length of the offer. Some restaurant chains hand out simulated coins or tokens redeemable for promotion. There is an added benefit to the cards and coins: Carried in the pockets or purses of the customers, they act as an advertising reminder.

DIRECT CONSUMER PROMOTIONS

Many relatively high-check ($15.00 or over) restaurants don't maintain customer mailing lists. True, the cost of promotion relative to the potential check can be a barrier. But using your present customer base, the people who have tried your restaurant and product and apparently like them, seems to make a good deal of sense. You are not asking the consumer to try the unknown. You are precisely targeting rather than scattergunning your promotion.

Promotions targeted toward specific groups of people inherently have a higher chance of proper response. Yet this is a truism ignored all too often in foodservice promotion. Further, there are many opportunities to profit from this type of targeting. Take senior citizens as an example of a target group. Previous research reveals the names and contacts of seniors clubs in your restaurant's area, and it should be easy to identify retirement housing developments. Churches and temples often organize clubs and activities for seniors. As for the group within the group, a seniors club might also include a bridge group planning an awards lunch. Another grouping that should work in many areas is local office workers, a natural way to build lunch time business. As for the group within the group, there may be a local business bowling league, which could offer an opportunity to build evening business.

If you can identify targets, you should be able to direct an appropriate type of promotion toward them. The most consistent methods of generating business from groups include the following:

- Distribute promotional materials directly to the group to increase awareness of your restaurant. A special offer or coupon should stimulate trial.
- Discounts should be made available to group members who present their group's ID or membership cards, or you can issue a VIP card that entitles holders to a discount.
- Make special arrangements to accommodate group events, such as "group nights," parties, monthly dinners, or meetings. You provide the dining area and perhaps a special discount or "preferred pricing."
- The group holds a party elsewhere and you provide what is needed, from bulk foods to full catering at a special rate.

The number of groups is almost infinite. Here are some of the more viable targets:

- Major businesses
- Churches and temples
- Sports teams/leagues
- Rotary/Kiwanis
- Youth clubs
- Health clubs
- Retailer groups
- College fraternities/sororities
- Police/fire departments
- City/county/state workers
- VFW/American Legion
- PTAs
- Schools
- Unions

Study each group to find the best applicable program or combination of programs. To review and expand on sound group promotional approaches and opportunities, consider the following:

- VIP discount cards
- Major employer payroll stuffer
- Student meal deals
- Resident discount
- Birthday parties
- Club member offer
- Specific promotion fliers with coupons

Some groups offer well-focused and specialized promotional opportunities when they attempt to raise funds for their own purposes. Fundraising events significantly increase the potential for group business and have the added benefit of involving your restaurant with the community and developing goodwill. You can tie in to the ongoing fundraising efforts with coupon books and fliers and, of course, you'll be on hand when the fundraising culminates in a dinner, which you can cater and during which your support will be recognized.

The chart in Figure 14.2 will aid in listing likely group business candidates and in keeping track of contacts.

Figure 14.2
FUNDRAISING / GROUPS

List appropriate fundraising organizations and social groups in your area (churches, schools, scouting groups, little leagues, etc.) Keep track of all activity with each group. When applicable, describe any promotion you do with them, and the results.

ORGANIZATION NAME & ADDRESS	PHONE #	CONTACT	COMMENTS

JOINT PROMOTIONS

Splitting the cost of an advertising message with a major supplier to your restaurant can often be friendly to both your budget and your image. Large companies often look on this type of joint promotion very favorably. Beverage companies, for instance, frequently will share in advertising costs if the advertising features their product prominently enough to increase brand exposure. Your own position will be enhanced by association with major firms.

Another form of joint promotion is cross-promotion, which involves having your units cooperate with other, noncompetitive retailers in your area. The essential feature of cross-promoting is that your unit distributes or displays material from the cooperating retailer, who does the same for you. Everybody tends to benefit, both retailers and customers, who can take advantage of two sets of discounts.

In setting up cross-promotions, the restaurant manager should be careful to recruit a partner who:

- Has a substantial customer count (supermarkets, department stores, movie complexes, gas stations, and sports arenas, for example).
- Maintains a quality operation. You want your name linked only with successful and well-regarded businesses.
- Is close to your restaurant. The location should be convenient for the customer.
- Is willing to cooperate in controlling and monitoring the promotion. Maximum return from a promotion requires accurate tracking, and you can't assume the entire responsibility for that by yourself.

MARKET SEGMENTATION

You will find many benefits in targeting promotions toward various segments of your business, often trying to avoid impact on other segments. A careful analysis of business trends will reveal where your optimal sales-building opportunities—and needs—occur. You should attempt to build your share of the following segments:

- Weekday
- Weekend

Figure 14.3
TACTICS

OPPORTUNITY AND PROGRAMS	INDIV	FAMILY	GROUPS	BRKFST	LUNCH	DINNER	LATE NITE	OTHER	WKDAY	WKEND	ALL
APT/CONDOS/SUB-DIVISIONS											
Discount Cards	X	X	X	X	X	X	X				X
Group Sales			X		X	X					X
Pool Parties (Picnics)		X	X		X					X	
FUNDRAISING/CHARITY (TIE-IN)											
Celebrity Partner	X	X	X	X	X	X	X				X
Toys for Tots	X	X		X	X	X	X				X
Gift Certificates	X		X	X	X	X	X	X			X
Promo Bucks	X		X	X	X	X	X	X			X
Elegant Evening		X				X		X			X
PLACES OF WORSHIP											
Fundraising	X	X	X	X	X	X					X
Windshield Fliers	X	X			X	X				X	
Large Orders			X		X	X					X
FAMILIES											
Family Feast		X				X					X
Picnics		X	X		X					X	
At Home Parties		X	X		X	X					X
SENIORS											
Coffee Club	X		X								
Senior Discount Card	X		X	X	X	X		X	X		X
Senior Pack	X				X	X					X
KIDS											
Birthday Parties		X	X		X	X					X
Kid's Meal Pack		X			X	X		X			X
BIRTHDAY CLUB											
Sign Up & Card	X	X		X	X	X					X
STORE ANNIVERSARY											
Price Roll back	X	X			X	X					X
1 cent or 5 cent sale	X	X			X	X	X				X
Free Item	X	X			X	X					X
PICNIC											
Complete Pack		X	X		X					X	X
LARGE ORDERS											
Quantity Discount		X	X		X	X	X				
FREQUENCY PROMOS											X
Lunch Club	X				X						
Dinner Club	X	X				X			X		X
EARLY BIRD DISCOUNT											XX
Happy Hours	X	X	X			X					XX
HOLIDAY									X		X
New Year's Day	X	X	X	X	X	X					
M.L King Jr., Day	X	X	X	X	X	X	X				
Lincoln 1 cent	X	X		X	X	X	X				
Valentine's Day	X	X		X	X	X	X				
Washington 25 cents	X	X		X	X	X	X				X
St. Patrick's Day	X	X	X		X	X	X				X
Easter		X		X	X	X				X	X
Mother's Day		X		X	X	X				X	X
Memorial Day		X	X		X	X				X	X
Father's Day		X		X	X	X				X	X
July 4th		X			X	X					X
Labor Day	X	X	X		X	X					
Halloween		X				X	X				X
Thanksgiving	X	X	X		X	X					
Christmas	X	X		X	X	X	X				X
New Year's Eve	X	X	X			X	X				
EVENT/TEAM SPONSORSHIP	X	X	X	X	X	X	X				
INTERSTATE								X			
Free Ice		X	X	X	X	X	X				
CREW SALES INCENTIVES											
Various	X	X	X	X	X	X	X				

OPPORTUNITY AND PROGRAMS	TARGET MARKET			MEAL PERIODS					WEEKPARTS		
	INDIV	FAMILY	GROUPS	BRKFST	LUNCH	DINNER	LATE NITE	OTHER	WKDAY	WKEND	ALL
OFFICES/FACTORIES/INDUS. PARKS											
Gofer Program			X		X				X		
Secretary's Week	X	X			X				X		
Large Order/Parties			X	X	X	X	X	X			X
Fast Serve Guarantee	X				X				X		
Payroll Envelope Stuffer	X			X	X				X		
Take a Friend to Lunch	X				X				X		
Business of the Week	X		X		X				X		
Take Dinner Home	X	X							X		
SHOPPING CENTERS/MALLS											
Employee Discount Card	X				X						X
Large Orders/Parties			X		X						X
Take Dinner Home	X	X									X
Late Night	X		X				X				X
Retail Tie-Ins	X	X			X	X	X				X
RETAIL OUTLETS (Cross-Promos)							X				
Coupon Exchange	X	X	X	X	X		X				X
VIDEO TIE-IN (Cross-Promo)							X				
Video Package	X	X	X				X	X			X
SERVICE STATIONS (Cross-Promos)							X				
Discount Coupons	X	X			X		X				X
HOTEL/MOTEL							X				
Welcome Flier/Coupon	X	X		X	X		X	X			X
REALTOR TIE-IN	X	X		X	X	X	X	X			X
BANK/DRIVE-THRU							X				
Discount Coupon	X	X			X						X
HOSPITALS							X				
Discount Card	X				X	X		X			X
Discount if in Uniform	X				X	X	X	X			X
Take Dinner Home	X	X				X					X
CLUBS/ORGANIZATIONS											
Discount Card	X		X	X	X		X				X
Large Order			X	X	X	X					X
Fundraisers	X		X	X	X						X
MOVIES/BOWLING ALLEYS											
Package Deal	X	X	X		X		X				X
Frequency Program	X	X			X	X	X				X
RECREATION PARKS							X				
Picnics		X	X		X					X	
Team Sponsorship	X	X	X		X		X				X
On-Location Sales	X	X			X	X				X	
SCHOOLS/COLLEGES											
Student Discount Card	X		X	X	X		X	X			X
Welcome Back Students	X				X	X	X	X			X
Large Orders (Dorms, Frats)			X		X	X	X				X
MILITARY							X				
Discount Card	X		X	X	X		X	X			X
Discount if in Uniform	X				X	X	X	X			X
STADIUMS/AUDITORIUMS							X				
After the Game	X	X	X				X	X			X
Tailgate Party		X	X		X	X					X
Event Special	X	X	X		X		X	X			X
CAR WASHES							X				
Cross-Promotion	X				X						X
PARKING LOT ACTIVITIES											
Flea Market/Sidewalk Sale	X	X			X					X	
Talent Shows	X	X			X					X	
Block Parties	X	X	X				X			X	
H.S. Band Concert		X	X			X					X
Gospel Sings		X	X								X
Car Wash	X	X			X				X	X	

Figure 14.1 (*continued*)

Figure 14.4
BUDGET SUMMARY

ADD THE COSTS FOR ALL PROMOTIONS SCHEDULED IN EACH MONTH
FROM THE PROMOTION BUDGET WORKSHEET, AND SUMMARIZE TOTALS HERE:

Market _____   Location _____   Year _____

MONTH	MEDIA (DISTRIBUTION COSTS) $	PRODUCTION $	MATERIALS $	TOTAL MARKETING $	SALES OBJECTIVE $	% OF SALES $
JAN.						
FEB.						
MARCH						
APRIL						
MAY						
JUNE						
JULY						
AUG.						
SEPT.						
OCT.						
NOV.						
DEC.						
TOTAL						

Figure 14.5
OBJECTIVES / STRATEGIES / TACTICS
(One sheet per month)

Market _____

Location _____

* MONTH _____

* SALES OBJECTIVE _____

* STRATEGIES

    # of customers _____

    $ per customer _____

* THE PROGRAMS I WILL IMPLEMENT TO ACHIEVE THE OBJECTIVE ARE:

1. Program Name: _____

   Timing: _____

   Budget: _____

   Notes: _____

2. Program Name: _____

   Timing: _____

   Budget: _____

   Notes: _____

3. Program Name: _____

   Timing: _____

   Budget: _____

   Notes: _____

Figure 14.6
SUMMARY OF OBJECTIVES / STRATEGIES

Market _____

Location _____

HERE ARE MY PLANNED SALES AND CUSTOMER LEVELS FOR THE 12-MONTH PERIOD:

MONTH	SALES	CUSTOMERS	$ PER CUSTOMER
JANUARY			
FEBRUARY			
MARCH			
APRIL			
MAY			
JUNE			
JULY			
AUGUST			
SEPTEMBER			
OCTOBER			
NOVEMBER			
DECEMBER			
TOTAL			

Figure 14.7
ANNUAL PROMOTIONAL ACTIVITY SCHEDULE

Market _____ Location _____ Year _____

PROMOTIONAL ACTIVITY	JAN.	FEB.	MARCH	APRIL	MAY	JUNE	JULY	AUGUST	SEPT.	OCT.	NOV.	DEC.

- Age Groups
- Early Week
- Breakfast
- Individual Customers
- Lunch
- Family Group
- Dinner
- Social Group

The trick is to craft your promotional methods to fit the specific needs of the market segment or segments you've selected for building. You'll find the chart in Figure 14.3 helpful in appropriately matching methods to segments, including specific audiences, meal periods, and weekparts. The methods themselves are grouped under opportunities programs. You'll want to copy these sheets for distribution so all your unit managers have them available for continual reference.

Figures 14.4–14.7 are fairly self-explanatory and will aid you in formalizing your promotions by month; in obtaining a yearly overview of target sales and customer levels; in creating an easy reference promotions calendar for the year; and in preparing a budget for your promotions by month and year.

CHAPTER HIGHLIGHTS AND REVIEW

1) Is each of your major and minor promotion events structured using the principle of vertical integration? Is each media tier included?

2) Are the communications disclaimers and disclosures clearly readable and understandable? Are they sufficient or too restrictive?

3) Have you integrated holiday themes—including the restaurant's anniversary—into the marketing plan as opportunities for promotion?

4) Are your promotion offers structured to meet the needs of the various demographic markets to which your concept appeals?

5) Have you incorporated up-selling and frequency building tactics at the point-of-sale for each promotion event?

6) Do you have a system in place for collecting your customers' names and addresses so you can communicate with them directly and easily?

7) Have you remembered to include in your plan programs, focused on individual trading area sales-building opportunities: groups, cross-promotions, and fundraisers?

8) Is your suggestive selling program well organized, and does it include effective management yardsticks? Are you trying to make salespeople out of people who aren't?

9) Is your complaint-handling program in place?

10) Do your marketing programs include appropriate publicity announcements to extend your consumer communications? Is the PR effort optimized?

11) Is each promotion presented in writing to clearly define its objective, description, support, responsibilities, and implementation details for all involved in its execution?

Chapter Fifteen

What Do I Pay?
What Do I Get?

As you have been reading the previous chapters, you've probably been hearing an inner voice of varying intensity asking something like, "How do I budget right for this?" or "How do I figure what effect one of these promotions really has on my sales?" This chapter will provide useful answers to both of these questions and several related ones as well.

THE BREAKEVEN INVESTMENT

There is a very practical formula for determining the extra sales needed to cover the expenses for a given marketing activity. This breakeven calculation consists of dividing the marketing expenditure by the marketing investment percentage—which is a good deal easier than it sounds. You find the investment percentage by deducting the total variable marketing expenses you anticipate from 100 percent, expressing each expense as a percentage of gross sales.

The following example, assuming $250 as the total invested in a given marketing activity, illustrates the formula:

Variable Expenses		*Calculation:*
Product Cost	30%	57% from 100% = 43%
Incremental Labor	10%	$250 divided by .43 = 581.40
Menu Price Discount	15%	
Supplies Estimate	2%	
Total Variable Expense	57%	

Using this example, you will need to generate $581.40 in extra sales to break even on the $250 investment. (*Note:* A franchised operation paying royalties and advertising contributions should add such percentages to the list of variables.)

Table 15.1 sets forth key information and mathematical formulas which will allow you to quickly determine the "break-even" point on any given marketing activity or promotion under consideration. To use this table effectively, follow these two simple steps:

1. Determine the % of each new dollar of revenues that should be attributed to variable expense (column 1). Calculate the proposed amount of dollars to be invested in a given marketing activity or promotion (column 3). For purposes of illustration, $100.00 is used as a standard on this table. For your purposes, simply substitute the actual investment amount in place of the $100.00 listed.

2. Multiply the pre-calculated breakeven sales factor (column 2) by column 3 to determine the amount of new revenues received to breakeven (column 4).

Table 15.1
Breakeven Sales Figures

Variable Expense % of Gross	Breakeven Sales Factor	Variable Expense % of Gross	Breakeven Sales Factor
35	1.54	100.00	154.00
36	1.56	100.00	156.00
37	1.59	100.00	159.00
38	1.61	100.00	161.00
39	1.64	100.00	164.00
40	1.67	100.00	167.00
41	1.69	100.00	169.00
42	1.72	100.00	172.00
43	1.75	100.00	175.00
44	1.79	100.00	179.00
45	1.82	100.00	182.00
46	1.85	100.00	185.00
47	1.89	100.00	189.00
48	1.92	100.00	192.00

Table 15.1 (*continued*)

Variable Expense % of Gross	Breakeven Sales Factor	Variable Expense % of Gross	Breakeven Sales Factor
49	1.96	100.00	196.00
50	2.00	100.00	200.00
51	2.04	100.00	204.00
52	2.08	100.00	208.00
53	2.13	100.00	213.00
54	2.17	100.00	217.00
55	2.22	100.00	222.00
56	2.27	100.00	227.00
57	2.33	100.00	233.00
58	2.38	100.00	238.00
59	2.44	100.00	244.00
60	2.50	100.00	250.00
61	2.56	100.00	256.00
62	2.63	100.00	263.00
63	2.70	100.00	270.00
64	2.78	100.00	278.00
65	2.86	100.00	286.00
66	2.94	100.00	294.00
67	3.03	100.00	303.00
68	3.13	100.00	313.00
69	3.23	100.00	323.00
70	3.33	100.00	333.00
71	3.45	100.00	345.00
72	3.57	100.00	357.00
73	3.70	100.00	370.00
74	3.85	100.00	385.00
75	4.00	100.00	400.00
76	4.17	100.00	417.00
77	4.35	100.00	435.00
78	4.55	100.00	455.00
79	4.76	100.00	476.00
80	5.00	100.00	500.00

EVALUATING THE PROMOTION

The proof of any promotion, of course, is in the magnitued of *new sales activity derived* from the promotion. In essence, how effective are your various marketing and promotional activities in generating a *true* increase in sales?

There is a formula for measuring the relative success of marketing activity on your business, a formula called "GRIF" (Growth Rate Impact Factor). This formula will provide an indicator of the activity's impact on your business and is a good starting point for judging the worth of the activity.

To fairly evaluate a given marketing activity or promotion's performance, you must first assess the sales increases on the basis of the pre-promotion sales trend. That is, what was the sales trend *before* the activity started? To do this, you must first separate the base period (*before* the activity began) and the evaluation period (*after* the activity was begun).

To illustrate, let's assume that a given promotional activity ran for a total of 4 weeks. This represents your *evaluation period.* Therefore, the 4 weeks *immediately preceding* is the base period. This approach, when viewed in the context of seasonal trends, allows you to identify given periods in prior years and logically compare prior year(s) results to current activity to judge the true effectiveness of any promotional activity in generating *real* new sales activity.

The following example demonstrates how the GRIF system can be used to evaluate a given promotional or marketing activity: The Mesquite Grill ran a Texas "Barbecue" promotion for a total of 4 weeks in the month of April. Therefore, August would be the evaluation period. The base period would be in March.

WEEKLY AVERAGES

BASE PERIOD				EVALUATION PERIOD			NET CHANGE
	Mar. Last Year	Mar. This Year	% Change	April Last Year	April This Year	% Change	
Sales	7500	7800	+4.0	8000	8800	+10.0	+6.0
Covers	938	963	+2.7	982	1073	+ 9.3	+6.6
$/Cover	8.00	8.10	+1.3	8.15	8.20	+ 0.6	−0.7

Figure 15.1
"GRIF" FORM

OUTLET _____   BASE PERIOD: From _____ To _____

MEAL PERIOD _____   TEST PERIOD: From _____ To _____

SALES ANALYSIS WORKSHEET

Category	Base Period			Test Period			Change Diff.
	Last Year	This Year	% Change	Last Year	This Year	% Change	
Sales							
Covers							
S/Covers							
Transactions							
Party Size							
S/Transactions							

Promotional Activity: _____

_____

_____

_____

Comments: _____

_____

_____

_____

The data shows that the change in sales during the evaluation period was +10 percent. But, since sales were already growing by 4% (the base period) going into the "Texas Barbecue" promotion, the promotion actually generated a net sales increase of 6%.six points of sales volume. A similar calculation indicates an increase, [FAX illegible], a net improvement of the cover count by +6.6%. Additional indicators that can be examined using "GRIF" include number of transactions, party size, and $ per transaction.

For example, if you wished to evaluate a gift certificate sales promotion (in addition to looking at total sales) you might examine the number of transactions and the $ per transaction to determine how many individual gift certificates were purchased, how many bulk certificate transactions took place, and the average $ value of the certificates sold.

The "GRIF" form in Figure 15.1 is provided for conducting such postpromotion evaluation analysis.

CHAPTER HIGHLIGHTS AND REVIEW

1) Calculate the dollar amount of extra sales you need to break even on promotional investment.

2) The Growth Rate Impact Factor (GRIF) formula provides a trustworthy indicator of a promotions impact on your business.

Chapter Sixteen

Do It Right or Forget It

All the positioning, brand personality development, and promotion planning you do won't mean a thing unless you've communicated them properly. Without the right communication, you don't get a chance to execute and to succeed.

ADVERTISING AND COMMUNICATIONS STRATEGY

Whether you rely on an advertising agency for the bulk of your media planning and purchasing, whether that responsibility falls primarily on in-house staff members, or whether it is shared by both groups, it's highly probable that when campaigns are presented to you they will consist of more glitz than guts.

This is because ad agencies are always in competition for business; your in-house staff wants to protect itself from outside agencies; and if the responsibility is shared, everyone wants to take the lion's share of the credit. Hence, the presentation often aims at *you* as the target rather than at *your market*.

Avoiding this situation is, like so many of the things discussed in this book, a matter of common sense, focus, and discipline. You need to exercise these traits in order to come up with consistent, targeted advertising and communications strategies. The real focus here is *who* are you trying to reach with *what message*.

The objective of advertising is to communicate a message to the target market (for example, that customers should visit XYZ outlet this week to try their lobster platter). The objective is a measurable statement around which the advertising is to be developed. The ad copy and graphics must communicate what the objective states.

Once the objective is developed, you then write your strategy. In some instances, ad agency personnel write the strategy and present it to you for approval. Sometimes the strategy is written by the client (you). Often it is a combined effort. Regardless of who does the actual writing, it is helpful to understand the ingredients of an effective communications strategy. An effective strategy states what you intend to convince the target market of, and provides support for that conviction. Advertising will convince a target audience, for example, that XYZ outlet is the best restaurant to get a lobster platter for a reasonable price for a short period of time. Support elements might look something like this:

- XYZ serves fresh, generous lobster platter meals
- XYZ serves the largest lobster in town (2 lbs.)
- By using a coupon, the price is $3 less than usual
- Offer is valid for only seven days

Use this checklist when developing your strategy for each new advertising development:

1) *Make your strategy easy to use.* Keep it short and sharp—one page at the most.
2) *Be single-minded.* Great ideas are simple.
3) *Agree on what's most important.* To consumers, some product characteristics are more important than others.
4) *Make meaningful promises.* Promise—large promise—is the soul of advertising.
5) *Support your promises with facts.*
6) *Communicate your brand personality to humanize your business.* Think of the advertisements for such products as Dr. Pepper, Johnson's Baby Powder, and Oil of Olay, and how clearly each brand's personality is communicated.
7) *Advertise what's important, not the obvious.*

YOUR ADVERTISING STRATEGY

The determination of who is in the market to buy (target audience) and the development of the action you desire the market to take (communications strategy) lead to the writing of your media strategy. The media strategy is used as the guide in the selection and purchase of media vehicles that will deliver your advertising message to the target audience(s). The strategy document details the relevant aspects of the communications strategy plus budget, timing, promotion offer (if any), and response device (e.g., coupon). (An example follows.)

Promotion Event: the introduction of a "Candlelight Dinner for Two" special, $29.95 per package, requiring the presentation of a coupon by the respondent. The package will be offered for a six-week period, October 10 through November 20, and the coupon will have a valid period of two weeks. The package is available seven nights per week.

Media Objective: to deliver to the target audience the sales message and the coupon in an effective and efficient manner. The six-week event will be considered a success when an average of 40 packages are purchased per night. Current users and new users should be attracted.

Media Strategy: This objective will be achieved by efficiently reaching the target audience in a timely, response-generating manner and within the framework of the established budget.

1) *The number of packages to be sold over the six-week period is 1,680 (42 nights × 40 packages).*
2) *The sales goal for the period (this special only) is $50,316 (1,680 × $29.95).*
3) *The media budget is planned at 5 percent of planned sales goal ($2,516).*
4) *Two target audiences need to be reached*—current users and new users.
5) *Coupons will carry two-week valid dates and will be of convenient size.*

With this strategy in hand, the next step is to select the media and to schedule the advertising dates. Certain media parameters are established. The selected media need to be coordinated with the design and copy approach of the creative materials to be used. In some instances, the media to be employed will dictate the creative development. In other instances, the creative materials will guide the media selection. Therefore, a coordinated effort is mandatory.

At this point, the media planner needs to possess a clear understanding of the available media options, their capability for delivering the sales message to the audience, and the associated costs of delivery. Further, the effectiveness of each medium must be considered.

If you have the services of an advertising agency available, providing the media strategy statement will be more than sufficient for the agency's media department to create an appropriate media plan for your approval. If you do not employ the services of an advertising agency, your job is to select, schedule, and purchase the media. Keep in mind

Figure 16.1
MEDIA INFORMATION SUMMARY

List the various media companies (i.e., radio stations, newspapers, direct mail houses) in your area. Note all pertinent information from their media kits: their format (i.e.,weekly or daily paper, Top 40 or Easy Listening radio), if they have zoned editions available (newspaper), and if you have trade (exchange of credit at your outlet for media space or time) set up with them. List the current rates (and the date these rates were filled in) for the type of ad you typically run with each media. Use this summary as a handy reference when preparing your marketing plan, but keep up-to-day media kits on file for any additional information.

Media/Company	Format	Contact	Notes

Figure 16.2
MEDIA CHARACTERISTIC RATINGS

	Media Characteristic	TV	Radio	Out-Door	Mkt. ROP	Free Local ROP	Paid Local ROP	Direct Mail 4/C Solo	Direct Mail 4/C Mar.	Direct Mail 2/C Mar.	Insert 4/C Solo	Insert 4/C Mar.	On Street 2/C	On Street 4/C	In-Unit 2/C	In-Unit 4-C
		1	2	3	4	5	6	7	8	9	10	11	12	13	14	15
A	Good Image Builder	Excel.	Good	Fair	Fair	Fair	Fair	Good	Fair	Fair	Good	OK	No	OK	Fair	Good
B	Creative Capacity	Excel.	OK	Fair	OK	OK	OK	Good	OK	OK	Good	Good	Fair	OK	OK	Good
C	Detailed Message	OK	OK	No	Good	Good	Good	Good	Good	OK	Good	Good	Good	Good	Good	Good
D	Commands Attention	Good	OK	Fair	OK	Fair	OK	Good	OK	OK	Good	OK	OK	Good	OK	Good
E	Lacks Ad Clutter	Good	Good	OK	No	Fair	Fair	Excel.	Fair	Fair	Good	Fair	Excel.	Excel.	Excel.	Excel.
F	Closed Promo Offer	Fair	Fair	No	Excel	Excel.	Excel.	Excel.	Excel.	Excel.	Excel.	Excel.	Excel.	Excel.	Excel.	Excel.
G	Reaches New Customers	Excel.	Excel.	Excel.	Excel.	Excel.	Excel.	Excel.	Excel.	Excel.	Excel.	Excel.	Excel.	Excel.	No	No
H	Reaches Current Customers	Excel.	Excel.	Excel.	Excel.	Excel.	Excel.	Excel.	Excel.	Excel.	Excel.	Excel.	Excel.	Excel.	Excel.	Excel.
I	Targetability	Fair	OK	Fair	Fair	OK	OK	Excel.	Good	Good	OK	OK	Excel.	Excel.	Excel.	Excel.
J	Reaches Mass Market	Excel.	OK	Fair	OK	No	No	No	No	No	OK	OK	No	No	No	No
K	Efficient Targeting	No.	Fair	No	Fair	OK	OK	OK	OK	Good	Fair	OK	OK	OK	OK	OK
L	Short Production Time	No	Good	No	Good	Good	Good	Fair	Fair	OK	Fair	Fair	Good	Fair	Good	Fair
M	Low Production Costs	No	OK	Fair	Good	Good	Good	Fair	Fair	OK	Fair	OK	Good	Fair	Good	Fair
N	Low Media Costs	No	OK	OK	Fair	Good	Good	No	OK	Good	No	OK	Excel.	Excel.	Excel.	Excel.
O	Low Cost Per 1,000	Excel.	OK	Excel.	OK	Good	OK	No	OK	OK	Fair	OK	OK	OK	Excel.	Excel.

Media Definitions

1. **TV** — 30 second, national quality spot
2. **Radio** — 60 second, national quality spot
3. **Outdoor** — Single painted board, near location
4. **Market Newspaper** — Quarter-page ad, national quality
5. **Local Newspaper** (Free distribution) — Quarter-page ad, national quality
6. **Local Newspaper** (Paid circulation) — Quarter-page ad, national quality
7. **Direct Mail** — 4c 2-sides single sheet, solo mailing
8. **Direct Mail** — 4c marriage mail—i.e., ADVO
9. **Direct Mail** — 2c marriage mail—i.e., VAL PAK
10. **Insert** — 4c 2-side free fall
11. **Insert** — 4c marriage—i.e., VALASSIS
12. **On-Street** — 2c flier
13. **On-Street** — 4c flier
14. **In-Unit** — 2c flier
15. **In-Unit** — 4c flier

Media Characteristics

Qualitative
A. **Good Image Builder—** has the capability of communicating a quality sales message in a quality presentation.
B. **Creative Capacity—** enables the writer/designer creative freedom.
C. **Can Deliver a Detailed Message—** has the capacity to preesnt a lengthy sales story.
D. **Commands Attention—** virtually forces involvement.
E. **Lacks Ad Clutter—** is presented without other ads fighting for attention.
F. **Can Deliver a Closed Promo Offer—** by employing a response device indicating ad response.

Quantitative
G. **Reaches New Customers—** has the capability of communicating to nonusers.
H. **Reaches Current Customers—** has the capability of communicating to current customers.
I. **Targetability—** allows selection of target markets.
J. **Reaches Mass Market—** has the capability of communicating to large numbers of potential consumers.
K. **Efficient Targeting—** reaches the target market at a relatively low cost.

Production/Costs
L. **Short Production Lead Time—** final execution for placement with the media is but a few days.
M. **Low Production Costs—** absolute out-of-pocket cost to produce is realtively low.
N. **Low Absolute Media Costs—** absolute cost to place media is relatively low.
O. **Low Cost Per 1,000 of Impressions—** the cost per 1,000 impressions is relatively low.

that ad agencies are paid by the media for their services, usually 15 percent of the media costs. You should consider the amount of time you will devote to this time-intensive process when deciding to use an agency or to do the work yourself. Whichever approach is taken, a working knowledge of the available media is necessary in order to place a schedule or to evaluate and approve an ad agency's media plan recommendation. (Figure 16.1 provides an example media information summary sheet.)

To provide you with this working knowledge, a summary of the various types of widely accepted media vehicles is provided in Figure 16.2.

WORKING WITH YOUR AD AGENCY

Sound relationships with your ad agency (if you use one) are crucial to the communications process that results in customers entering and reentering your restaurant. Too many people, however, don't recognize the substantial benefits to be gained in staying with the same advertising agency for a number of years. Unfortunately, most clients never realize those benefits because they either dump the agency or are dumped after only a year or two.

Just as many ad campaigns are abandoned before they reach full potential, many client-agency relationships are not allowed to grow. Although these delicate relationships may be ended for some very valid reasons, many fall victim to the following hazards, either singly or in combination:

The Us/Them Syndrome. This is only natural during the selection and negotiation phases, but once the agreement is signed it's got to become "WE" for the relationship to work.

Poorly defined roles and responsibilities. Failure to assign key functions clearly usually leads to unrealistic expectations, missed deadlines, and lack of enthusiasm for what ought to be creative and rewarding work.

Failure to educate the agency in the client's business. Good advertising is built on knowledge, and that comes from hands-on experience, hard work, and cooperation.

The following guidelines equip the foodservice advertiser to build a strong, continuing ad agency relationship:

- Make the agency an informed partner by sharing as much information as possible (customer demographics, competitors and their promotions, average check, key menu items).
- Set specific, measurable objectives.
- Set a budget, but be prepared to adjust the budget if that's what it takes to accomplish the goal.
- Work with the agency to develop a strategy that's right for the business.
- Define a specific target or prospect group (e.g., adults aged 25–49 with household income of $30,000 or more, living within five miles of the location).
- Define the "reason why" people will visit the outlet (in general or for a promotion). This is your point-of-difference in your mission statement, it is what sets you apart.
- Give the agency your "mandatories" and policy limitations up front (i.e., logo use, address). Do not try to "tack" these on the end.
- Give and get specific due dates for each step of the project.
- Get estimates before spending money.
- Invite agency staff to eat at your restaurant. You will show them your products, and they will have the opportunity to get their "creative juices" flowing in a less formal environment.
- Let the agency do the creative work. If you have a creative execution in mind, communicate it—but always tactfully. Creative people are very sensitive and like to come up with their own ideas. However, your ideas may be right on target. Communicate these in a way that allows the agency to more fully develop or improve on the idea. After setting objectives and providing all appropriate background, suggest "how about something like . . . " Then, remember that you're paying for the agency's creative expertise.

Since ad agency fees are based primarily on the amount of time budgeted for working on a client's business, the client should make sure these costly agency hours are being spent in the best way possible. An agency should be used to:

Write new copy for advertising
Develop ongoing campaigns
Come up with winning headlines
Recommend media

Design and develop four-color print materials

Create new advertising

Typeset advertisements, headlines, or body copy

Produce broadcast advertising

Develop the "Master" or the first version of a new piece such as a monthly calendar

Be cautious when a publication offers to set type for you. This is usually free, but remember, you get what you pay for. Your agency can deliver a better product.

In general, don't use the advertising agency to:

Change a few words of factual copy on advertisements or merchandising pieces (new price, date, menu item)

Produce straightforward printing jobs, such as reprinting fliers

Plan or execute public relations (unless they have a separate department)

Use this advertising checklist in Table 16.1 to make sure your advertising dollars yield sales dollars.

Table 16.1
Advertising Checklist

1. Positioning—vital for success
2. Promise—attractive and meaningful
3. Continuity—don't give up
4. Big Idea—motivating
5. Go First Class—appearance is everything
6. Consumer Benefit—give 'em a reason
7. Lead, Don't Follow—make it your own
8. Create Excitement—think big, be a showperson
9. Target the market—sell
10. Do Research—the foundation of solid communications

Epilogue

When I decided to write this book, some time had passed since that Friday night flight home to Florida. In fact, a lot of things have happened since then: The Berlin Wall has crumbled; victory was achieved in the Persian Gulf; the country struggled with a recession. But what has not changed is the fact that many foodservice industry executives remain complacent and fail to respond to competitive challenges.

The months between that flight and the publication of this book have not changed my convictions either. A well-structured and well-executed marketing plan is essential to success in the foodservice industry. The competition for the foodservice dollar is fiercer than ever. And there are many changes in the industry that challenge foodservice providers.

As the nineties began, a solid consensus grew among hospitality and foodservice people that the days of relying on catchy slogans, zippy jingles, and flashy nationwide campaigns were fading, and fading fast. There is a more profitable way to spend the advertising dollar: Start with the local unit.

An industry operations survey by the National Restaurant Association revealed that nearly one of every five visits to a fast food or family restaurant involved some type of price discount or coupon promotion.

It's noteworthy that foodservice industry spending on local television is also on the rise. TGI Fridays and Denny's, for example, have increased local radio expenditures more than 100 percent since 1987.

Top marketers are again looking for in-store neighborhood-oriented marketing for survival. Children's segment marketing is one facet of this type of promotional consideration. Get the kids and you get their families. So we enter this decade with a reaffirmation of a long-held industry truth: The battle is between outlet and outlet, much more than between chain and chain.

This book gives you the right marketing system to take advantage of the opportunities of the nineties. And, despite the gloom-and-doomers, there are real opportunities. But you have to approach them positively and spread your positive attitude throughout your organization.

Glossary

ADI (area of dominant influence)   Geographic area of counties in which an advertiser's market television stations hold a dominance of total hours viewed. ADI tells the advertiser the size of the market reached by local stations.

Bounceback certificate or coupon   A coupon often good for a product offer on a return visit and possibly good only for another meal period. Customer is "bounced back" to the outlet. Used to increase frequency of current customer's visits.

Brand personality   Psychological bond that exists between the foodservice provider and its customers—or the emotional attachment and perceptions of consumers.

Buyer behavior   Way customers balance prices and satisfaction within the limits of the amount of money they have to spend.

Co-op mail/Mail   Targeted direct response pieces of several advertisers grouped together in the same distribution package. The direct response pieces are coupons/offers that are frequently put into envelopes or bound together and sent through the mail.

Community involvement   Programs designed to tie in elements in the community to benefit it and to enhance the image of the outlet.

CPP (cost per point)   Budgeting method used by most agencies to obtain an advertising level at a predetermined cost (for example, 100 rating points per week at $50 CPP = $5,000 budget per week).

Demographics   Various subgroups into which a total population (i.e., all customers of a food and beverage outlet) can be segmented. Demographics will include the numbers or percentages of the total group classified according to sex (male or female), race (black, white, Hispanic, Indian, etc.), or income (under $100,000; $10,000–$15,000; $15,000 and over, etc.), or other classifications.

Direct mail   Advertising mailed directly and frequently designed to generate response by asking the customer to bring in a coupon. These mailings are accomplished through the use of mailing addresses selected by geographic area, demographics, or both.

Flight   Period of an advertiser's campaign or the period in which a series of related ads in the same medium is run, followed by a period of inactivity (for example, an ad run during a specific selling season).

Flier   Informational piece sometimes including a discount, within the outlet's immediate trade area. It is specifically designed to build awareness, to encourage trial and retrial, and to broaden the existing customer base.

Four-color printing   Printing that employs the three primary colors plus black to give a full-color reproduction.

Frequency   Total number of times your target audience will see or hear your message within a given period. This number is usually given as an average frequency per week. (In research, frequency usually means frequency of visit.)

Fringe   Time periods preceding or following the prime time television period of 8 P.M.–10 or 11 P.M.

GRP (gross rating point)   Total estimated size of the television or radio audience for a given program (or advertisement), expressed as a percentage of the total audience, in terms of either households or individuals. GRPs include duplication. The relationship among reach (R), frequency (F), and gross rating points (GRPs) is expressed by the formula: $R \times F = GRPs$.

Hiatus   Break or gap between flights; period of inactivity between advertising flights.

Market   Group of patrons or households with similar characteristics, wants, needs, buying power, and willingness to spend for dining and drinking out. (ADIs are also referred to as markets.)

Marketing   Manner and means by which you expose your outlet to the public.

Marketing mix   Combination of "the four Ps": product (food, menu, atmosphere), price, promotions/advertising, and place (location, site).

Marketing objectives   Measurable, achievable, and reasonable goals that your marketing efforts are intended to accomplish.

Marketing perspective   Placing the consumer's satisfaction first in all planning, objectives, policies, and operations. Since profitable sales volume is contingent on customer satisfaction, concentration should be on the patrons and sales volume will reflect their degree of satisfaction.

Marketing policy   Predetermined course of action to be followed as long as recurring conditions exist.

Market research   Information gathered about property, product, and/or market. May be subdivided into primary data (direct questioning of consumers for a specific project) or secondary data (collected through another source and indirectly related to the project).

Marketing segmentation   Dividing the total market into smaller homogeneous submarkets or segments.

Marketing strategy   Overall plan of action for each component of the marketing mix that enables the outlet to reach a predetermined objective.

Marketing   Programs designed to counteract problems and exploit the opportunities for any outlet (implementing the strategy of the objective).

Media   Any of the various types of advertising vehicles that can be used to deliver advertising messages. Television, radio, newspaper, outdoor posters, and skywriting are all considered media.

Media merchandising   Use of tradeout agreements, cooperative promotions, and bonus spots in negotiation with radio and television stations as a substitute for all or a portion of a purchased schedule.

Menu mix   Full list of menu items from which patrons may make selections and the corresponding percent of units sold or sales dollars generated for each item.

Neighborhood marketing   Series of disciplined advertising, promotional, and public relations activities to increase awareness, traffic, and sales in an outlet's trading area.

Net profit   Profit realized after all product costs, operating expenses, and promotional expenses have been deducted from the net sales of the item during the time of the promotion. Net profit is the criterion used in measuring the success of a promotion.

Outdoor   Advertising on signs of various kinds, such as posters, painted bulletins and billboards, and vehicles.

POS (point-of-sale) materials   Signs, displays, posters, table tents, mobiles, and countercards that make up the package of promotional materials displayed in a food and beverage outlet. Sometimes called POP (point of purchase).

Positioning   Written statement of the outlet's "reason for being," formulated to provide a base on which day-to-day operations are conducted and decisions are made. The positioning statement denotes what a foodservice provider is, where it wants to be, and where it is going.

Problems and opportunities Negative and positive characteristics within your outlet's trading area that hinder or encourage sales growth (also referred to as strengths/weaknesses).

Promotion Activities of a certain nature aimed to evoke a specific response from a customer—to buy a specific item, to enter a sweepstakes, to redeem a coupon, or to visit an outlet.

Promotional radio Negotiating with a radio station in order to obtain free, live, on-air mentions or bonus spots in exchange for product.

Publicity Gaining of public attention through newspapers and news broadcasters by providing information or conducting an event or activity that has news value. Activities you conduct in an outlet may have the potential for good publicity (i.e., charity donations).

QSC Quality of product, speed of service, and cleanliness of the food and beverage outlet.

Rating Percentage of people or households in a specific area watching or listening to a particular program. Ratings are usually expressed in terms of points. Thus, a proposed commercial for a specific time period may deliver 7 rating points. This means that the spot is reaching 7 percent of the total households. When you add up all the rating points in your media plan over a specified period of time, you obtain your gross rating points.

Reach Percentage of people in your target audience who will see or hear your advertising message. A high reach over a four-week radio flight can deliver 60 percent of your audience. A low reach will be in the 20 percent category.

ROI (return on investment) Incremental sales dollars divided by total costs.

ROP (run of paper/run of press) Placement of an advertisement anywhere within the publication that the publisher elects (normally, a nonpreferred position).

Situation analysis Combining the physical characteristics, location, and sales information of your food and beverage outlet, this do-it-yourself study also includes the demographics and physical characteristics of the property's trade area. It is used as a guide to determine traffic generators and problems/opportunities for neighborhood marketing purposes.

Solo insert Page printed by the advertiser and inserted into a magazine or newspaper by the publisher. It is often printed on different stock than that used by the publication. It is used for broad reach/awareness.

Spot Commercial announcement time available for sale or purchase from local radio or television stations by advertisers to air their commercials.

Success factors Activities in which an operation or company must excel in order to compete and earn a profit.

Systems approach Implementing the marketing concept through a fully integrated management effort.

TRP (target rating point) Representative of 1 percent of a particular target audience, TRPs define the target audience much more specifically than GRPs. For example, to have your message aim at males 25 to 54 years of age, you would have to use TRPs.

Tie-ins Cooperative or joint venture promotions involving your outlet and another retailer or organization with the desired end result being increased business.

Trading area Geographic area from which most of a specific outlet's customers are coming. This area will vary in size and shape, depending on the drawing power, type of restaurant, and other factors.

Traffic Place, business, or organization in your trading area where people congregate for whatever reason. Shopping malls, work offices, recreation areas, schools, and churches can be traffic generators.

Vertical integration Principle of integrating the same message into all marketing communications.

Appendix A

Direct Mail

Direct mail has been the premier advertising medium for the restaurant industry for many years. It has survived attempts to replace it simply because it is so effective in generating sales. But direct mail continues to be challenged, with its very longevity sometimes used as an argument against it. The following time-tested advantages of direct mail counter these challenges:

Measurement—You can achieve greater measured results.

Flexibility—You can be as expansive as you wish or your mailings can be tailored to concise interests.

Selectivity—You can zero in on almost any target audience and eliminate costly exposures to marginal audiences.

Personalization—You can use your name in any number of ways. You can also highlight your interests, whether you mail to a consumer or businessperson.

Response—Direct mail usually achieves the highest percentage of response per 1,000 people reached of any other advertising medium.

Testing—You can only do limited testing in other media, but with direct mail you have an unlimited opportunity to test so you can acquire information on product acceptability, pricing, audiences, offers, copy approaches, and so on.

Profit Possibilities—A customer acquired by mail remains a mail-oriented customer and can be sold to again and again, often without expensive sales calls, by using highly targeted and inexpensive direct mail promotions.

Extensive Reach—You may think your company is too small to compete with the giants. Direct mail, however, is the great equalizer.

To make sure you maximize promotional mileage and competitive edge in your direct mail campaigns, keep these execution tips in mind:

1) The most important element is the list. An excellent offer with a striking carrier and compelling copy, if mailed to the wrong list, can be a disaster.

2) Direct mail is a demanding taskmaster. If it fails, it's probably you who missed somewhere, not the medium. If possible, "test" some or all portions of your program so you can alter methods if needed.

3) Closely analyze your potential markets and your offer so you can hone lists and copy to target your approach.

4) Incorporate an action device (coupon, order form, reply card or envelope, phone number). Make it easy for the recipient to take the desired action.

5) A letter almost always pulls better in making a direct mail package more effective. Don't worry if the letter repeats information presented elsewhere in the package. The sales letter is a one-to-one communication to explain and sell, to get the recipient to act.

6) Study all elements of your package so you can know what is working. Is it the price? The geography? The timing? The phrasing of the offer? The list? The copy? The product? Which of these myriad elements makes the critical difference in the return?

7) People who take action by mail are different from those who don't. The best lists are of mail buyers of similar products or services who recently purchased in the same price range.

8) Do what is necessary to make your mail stand out, even "look peculiar," since it has to fight all types of competition. Clever "teaser copy" on the outside can work wonders.

9) Wise mail merchants work at differentiating among "suspects," "prospects," and "customers." Keep good records of what happens and when it happens with mailings to a particular list with a particular offer.

10) Testimonials can be effective promotional tools. Treat testimonials like the jewels they are and gather more.

11) There is no such thing as a "normal" percentage of return that's universally applicable across a wide range of products or services, but over time and by keeping careful records, you can determine some norms for your offer(s).

12) "Nothing is as simple as it seems." In producing direct mail programs, these seven words may be a cliche—but only because they're true! Continued care needs to be exercised at every step of the planning and conceptual stage and the production process.

Healthy Corporate Planning: A Structure for Strategic Planning

Twenty years ago, you might have been able to put a useful business plan together without strategic planning. That is not possible today. The very essence of growth is change. How can you know change has taken place without looking at both the past and the future?

In creating a healthy corporate plan, the availability of high technology could tempt you to overuse analytical models and quantifiable data. These are useful tools but only after you put your experience and gut feelings to work to make sense of the results. The enticement is strong to use these methods in the absence of strategic planning and to fool yourself into thinking your planning process is complete. To avoid this pitfall, you should include high-tech data to support your goals but not vice-versa.

The awareness of a need for "high touch," on the other hand, could encourage endless meetings and discussions in the absence of analytical data. The temptation here is to avoid analyzing the results of the planning process and to fool yourself into thinking that the planning is founded in reality. You have to be able to think strategically before you can plan strategically.

The whole point of a healthy corporate planning session is to fully merge both worlds—to use both quantifiable data and opinions/feelings. Strategic planning can be very useful in and of itself. Its whole point is to bring convergence among executives and board members about why the company exists and where it should be heading, and to create honest values, missions, and goals.

In strategic planning, it is the process that counts. A good product flows from a good process. That's why you must pay close attention to the participants, structure, and flow of your planning session.

Every group or person who has veto power over your business activities and who has made use of that power must be included in the strategic planning session. The worst kind of veto power is benign neglect flowing from passive-aggressive attitudes. Be sure to get even vocal leaders and opinion makers involved. Resist the temptation to leave out a trouble-maker. The whole point of the strategic planning session is to bring out different points of view so they can be addressed and moved toward a convergence of vision. Even if participants exercise addictive or sabotaging behavior styles, it is still more important to have them present than to have a smoother session. The most successful planning sessions are those in which there is a lot of disagreement and controversy. It is the discussion, along with the give and take of forthright people, that assures that the interest and views of the customers will be voiced. Look at the differing opinions as a resource, not a threat, and don't be afraid to invite comment.

It is critical that no board member, manager, or CEO run the meetings or dominate them. This can be prevented only by choosing a trained, assertive facilitator who will control the session without being obtrusive. Running a strategic planning session without an outside facilitator is rarely successful for several reasons.

First, regardless of an insider's attempt to act objectively, there is always the danger that that individual will be perceived as running a personal agenda or bowing to an aggressive opinion maker in the group. Second, if the insider is good, you need that person as a participant, not an objective bystander. Third, an insider's experience as a facilitator is often more limited than a professional's so the process developed for the meeting may reflect too narrow a view of strategic planning.

During strategic planning sessions, time should always be dedicated to discussion of the past, the present, and the future. Some facilitators spend too little time on the past, believing that strategy is being formulated for the future. In a way, that is correct, but they're also assuming that everyone knows why your business exists and what it's all about. Remember: The best lessons come from past mistakes when you finally understand why they happened.

To plan where you want to go, it's necessary to know where you are. That's why every strategic planning session must include data on the present. If someone says it's too boring or they don't understand how the current report relates, then they must be educated. Otherwise their ignorance will be a millstone around the necks of the rest of the planners. Anyone who doesn't understand the current position has no business voicing opinions about the future.

The future is often the fun part of strategic planning. More opinions will be given during this part of the planning process than at any other time. That's fine and that's the way it should be. All efforts should be made to encourage even the most reticent participants to share their vision of the future. Since the degree of consensus about the future is directly correlated to the degree of consensus about the past and present, spend ample time on the first two stages. Be careful not to get bogged down in tactics.

To allow enough time for the strategic planning session, try to plan a weekend retreat where nothing can interrupt the process. At the very least, the session should be an all-day affair, with a commitment from all parties involved to stay with it from beginning to end. It is deadly to the planning process to let anyone come late or leave early. People arriving late will dampen the enthusiasm and mood of the session.

The steps outlined below are an example of a planning session format called "Exploiting the Inevitable." It is designed to get the board and management team moving in the same direction by emphasizing that external pressures will inevitably affect their business, whether they like it or not. Productivity is often a goal that relies as much on external variables as it does on internal variables. Frequently, this means understanding how exterior competitive and noncompetitive variables you cannot control may affect your business.

Break the group up into four smaller teams, maintaining a mix of management and board members. You may wish to designate one team as finance, one as operations, one as marketing, and one as human resources. Periodically during the session, these teams will meet to brainstorm issues and then report back to the larger group.

To exploit the inevitable, it's necessary to understand the company's past and all the factors that will affect its future. The first step focuses on creating a common understanding of the company's history and what should be factored into any future plans. Three subparts of this first phase are the company's "stakeholders," its strengths, and its weaknesses.

A stakeholder is any individual, group, or organization that is affected by or has an impact on your company. This includes such entities as financial institutions, regulators, and customers. The first brainstorming session is meant to identify stakeholders and has three stages. To start, give each team five minutes to devise a list of generic groups of stakeholders (level-one stakeholders) such as government, financial institutions, and local businesses. The teams then reconvene and share their lists, blending the four lists into one master list.

Divide the teams again, supplying each with a copy of the master list (either all of it or a quarter of it), from which they are to develop a list of level-two stakeholders, specific entities within the generic groups identified in level one. Once again, bring the four teams together to share lists. When everyone understands and identifies the various entities, each member prioritizes the list.

Next, everyone lists the entities and rates them on a scale of 1 (not important) to 5 (very important). You may be surprised at the number of stakeholders identified. For instance, a board member from one firm remarked after this exercise that he had a whole new appreciation for the CEO—who had to contend with 133 stakeholders.

Having identified stakeholders and their relative importance to the company, the focus now turns to strengths and weaknesses. This is done in two stages, focusing first on strengths and then on weaknesses. Follow the routine used for identifying stakeholders, dividing into teams and then reporting back to develop a comprehensive list. Allocate time for explaining items on the lists, when necessary, but limit the explanations so there are no long, drawn-out dissertations. You'll find that putting the strengths and weaknesses on a flip chart goes a long way toward tuning everyone's thoughts.

Brainstorming on the company's stakeholders, strengths, and weaknesses will articulate its past in a surprisingly efficient and noncontroversial way.

The next part of the strategic planning session is the present. Oddly enough, the first stage here is envisioning the future. What you do in the present is strongly influenced by your views of the future. The visioning exercise consists of two steps taken by each of your four teams.

The first step is to envision the company's environment in five years. This involves consideration of political and economic trends at local, state, and national levels as well as of your consumers, suppliers, and channels. The second step of the visioning exercise is how the firm will fit in that environment. For example, two team members could prepare a worst-case scenario while the others prepare a best-case scenario. The exercise should end with a comprehensive expression of what the entire planning group wants the corporation to look like five years from now.

At this point, the planners have considered stakeholders, strengths, weaknesses, a vision of the future environment, and the company's place in it. Now, these will all be taken together to formulate ideas and concerns about the company and its direction. These individual ideas and concerns, if handled correctly, will be a piece of cake! Everyone will have had an opportunity to get an issue on the table.

The next stage of the strategic planning process is to examine what the company should be about, to formulate a more dynamic role in the strategic planning process, and to create a statement of philosophy for discussion purposes. Don't spend a lot of time looking for nonoffensive words (e.g., "service" instead of "profits") or making sure the phrasing is all-encompassing. The point of this exercise is to discuss the philosophy of your business and how it is revealed day by day, and to provide a single focus for your corporate culture. Each team is then charged with preparing two mission action statements for the coming year. Don't worry about precise wording here either. An example of a mission action statement for the finance group might be, "Have a financially sound business." Mission action statements are dynamic, responding to the issues facing the company in the coming year. Their broad, generic nature, however, necessitates that they ultimately feed into strategies. The next phase of the strategic planning session, therefore, is to reduce the mission action statements to strategies with clearly defined due dates and to name the key managers responsible for their accomplishment.

At this point, the immediate future should be addressed. The stakeholders, the strengths and weaknesses, the visions of the future, the concerns of the group regarding the company, and, finally, the philosophy that underlies the business's activities constitute the data bank from which mission statements emerge and out of which objectives, goals, and strategies are formed. Participants should now be ready to work toward developing the strategy for the coming year's operation.

Since each team has identified two mission action statements for its respective area, the next step is to develop objectives for these mission action statements. The individual teams do this by brainstorming all the possible roadblocks to accomplishment. For example, the financial mission action statement—Have a financially sound business—may encounter some roadblocks, such as cost overruns on employee wages and benefits. It is important that the group stay with the brainstorming and develop a comprehensive list of all the things that could block fulfillment of the mission action statement.

Once the list of roadblocks is completed, you will look at those roadblocks as opportunities. The entire group now turns its attention to developing solutions. The first step is to list each roadblock and discuss pertinent solutions. The roadblock of wage and benefit cost overruns might be solved, for example, by accurate weekly reports of employee costs, development of a functional cost analysis for each position, and cost justification for each proposed new position. These solutions, once identified, are listed as objectives. You will then prioritize the objectives, particularly if they are numerous.

The next step is to discuss each objective and list specific goals for the objective. The goals are quantified when possible, carry a target date for completion and designate a specific person as responsible for implementation. For example, the objective of developing a functional cost analysis of each position could result in a goal like, "The accounting department will research and propose a functional cost analysis program to the CEO by March 1. The person in charge of this goal will be the controller." It is not necessary that the goals be articulated in such detail as to specify the purpose of the strategy, the last part of strategic planning.

It is good management practice not to pursue strategies in the strategic planning meeting. The company has hired talented managers and a CEO to accomplish goals within their areas of responsibility. In fact, it is sometimes recommended that the strategic planning session end with the mission action statements, allowing the management team to continue developing objectives, goals, and strategies. The board's time restraints and expertise should influence the degree of board involvement in objectives and goals, but the implementation should definitely be left to the respective managers. Their strategies, however, should be reported back to the CEO.

Each goal, then, should have a strategy, a way to accomplish it. An example of part of the strategy for the goal, "The accounting department will research and propose a functional cost analysis program to the CEO by March 1" would be "Sue will contact software vendors and compile a list of appropriate computer programs by January 15." The strategies become a recipe for the accomplishment of the goal. They should be detailed enough so that if anyone in the department followed the strategy, the goal would, in fact, be accomplished.

There are some things to be careful of when developing strategies. After writing the strategy, make sure you can answer the question, "How do I know if I've achieved it?" For example, you may have a strategy stating that "There will be effective control of overtime." How do you know when you will have accomplished this? Does effective control of overtime mean no overtime, half of last year's overtime, the same level of overtime as last year or what? Who is to control this, and how? A better strategy statement is: "Supervisors will be charged with monitoring overtime and reporting it to the operations officer on a weekly basis so that steps can be taken to keep overtime below last year's level by hiring a part-time employee."

Sometimes strategies are criticized as belaboring the obvious. One reason for this criticism is the lack of precise wording in expressing what is to be accomplished and when. Words like "ongoing," "adequate," and "effective" are too vague for strategic planning statements. For example, it is obvious that "Employees should have an ongoing attitude of pleasantness that adequately reflects hospitality to customers in such a way that effective service is rendered." This statement, however, is not very useful to strategic planning. On the other hand, consider the statement "A seminar on customer relations will be conducted at the beginning of each quarter. Employees will attend the seminar to improve service." This statement is more informative and useful. It is a strategy while the previous statement is more like an objective.

Every strategy should be related to a goal, which is related to an objective, which is related to a mission action statement. It is advisable to code or letter the strategies according to their originating mission statement so they can always be defended, partly on the merit of those statements.

This process of developing strategy has finally brought us into the realm of the business plan, where strategies become an important element of the plan. The annual business plan is reality—an operating plan rather than something you take to the bank to borrow money. It can be reduced in complexity and detail for fundraising. Both documents will be effective if they reflect a comprehensive perspective on marketing issues.

Before you move on to the business plan, however, remember that in strategic planning, it is the process that's critical. Everything that's produced in a strategic planning session should be viewed as dynamic and subject to change. If you've really worked through the process, which improves with experience, however, a good strategic plan will stand the test of time. Subtle changes may be required. It is the execution and tactics that may require major revision. In fact, the process is so critical and dynamic in today's changing environment that businesses should conduct strategic planning sessions every six months.

Appendix C

New Products =
New Profits—
Or Do They?

No discussion of foodservice marketing is complete without coverage of the techniques of introducing new menu products. New products, properly handled, represent the biggest single traffic builder in the foodservice industry. Moreover, given the fact that the days when sales and market share could be substantially expanded by simply building new locations are long gone, new products present the most reliable path to expansion.

The demographic shifts mentioned at the beginning of this book have created several promising areas for development of new menu products. These include breakfast foods, light or nutritious foods, new taste experiences (regional or ethnic items), foods not easily prepared at home, takeout food, and delivered foods. These areas have been opened up by the demands of customers who are older, better educated, more convenience-oriented, and more nutritious- and weight-conscious than restaurant customers of the past. And each area offers its own special advantages to restaurant operators. Breakfast, for instance, is an opportunity for incremental sales and can be prepared on existing equipment. The demand for more nutritious and reduced-calorie foods suggests menu additions such as salads, baked or broiled items, and pastas.

American consumers' desire for new tastes creates a ready-made market for ethnic and regional specialties. As people become more habituated to simplified cooking at home (microwave and frozen dishes), they look to restaurants for items that take longer to prepare. Takeout and delivery of foods expand sales without significant negative effect on current traffic.

Similarly, each of the three basic types of new food products—entrees, side dishes, and new-category products—plays its own role on the menu.

The new entree should expand the menu without departing from the restaurant's fundamental concept. It rounds out and maintains the menu's competitiveness, particularly when it matches a competitor's offering. The McDLT, for example, was added to defend McDonald's menu against the B-K Whopper. The goal for the entree is to bring in new customers,, to increase the average ticket by trading up customers and to increase the frequency of visits by extending variety. The purpose of a new side dish is to increase the average check and to differentiate an operation from its direct competitors. Popeye's corn on the cob and KFC's baked beans are examples. New-category products are outside the scope of the restaurant's current menu and address important consumer needs that have not yet been met. Wendy's baked potatoes and Church's catfish are examples.

If any additional confirmation of the desirability of considering new menu items is needed, just take a look at what the major chains have been doing over the past few years: Burger King's breakfast buddies, burger buddies, and Chicken Tenders; Wendy's chicken cordon bleu, bacon swiss burger, and chicken nuggets; McDonald's hot dog nugget, breakfast biscuits, and Chicken McNuggets; Kentucky Fried Chicken's Hot 'n Spicy and chicken nuggets; and Church's Crispy Nuggets and southern catfish.

In this brief list, you can see evidence of both real innovations and "follow-the-leader" items. The innovations are aimed specifically at expanding a company's market, while following the leader is usually the route to preserving market share by providing a product similar to the competition's offerings.

What is most visible about the introduction of such new menu items is the costly advertising that surrounds their rollout. The Croissan'wich and new Whopper campaign cost nearly $50 million, Wendy's breakfast menu intro ran $14 million, and Church's reportedly spent $5 million to introduce catfish to regional markets. Yet new product development and introduction can be reasonably priced. Restaurant firms of all sizes can and should be prepared to put new items on their menus and advertise them on an appropriate scale. One of the keys to controlling menu development and advertising costs, of course, is discipline. Discipline is also critical to the success of a new product—whatever type of area of opportunity best classifies it.

Although it will vary in detail from firm to firm, the following product development process should be standard practice for the foodservice industry.

Step 1: Product Identification. Selection can spring from a variety of sources, including competitors, operations management, corporate staff, or a specially assigned task force. Sophisticated marketers, of course, conduct consumer research when they are deciding whether to introduce a new product. But it doesn't really matter where the idea comes from. It is more important that it is right for the business and that it ultimately has a positive impact on sales and profits.

It may be just as well to start with a substantial number of product ideas and work by elimination to identify the best ones. Screening these ideas effectively normally involves both qualitative and quantitative analysis. Qualitative analysis entails answering a series of pertinent, open-ended questions about each proposed menu idea. Quatitative analysis rates the product numerically.

The worksheet in Figure C.1 is useful in qualitative analysis. The focus of this exercise is to shed light on how the product will meet company priorities. It will answer a number of meaningful questions, including:

- Will the new product affect one meal period more than others? If so, which one?
- Will the new product increase customer counts or trade up the customer? What are realistic goals for these increases? Which sales and profit targets are realistic?
- What kind of customer will the new product attract, and at what price? (Setting a general target price will forestall creating a product with a price that is too high for the target customer. It also helps set guidelines for food costs.)
- What weaknesses and threats will work against it? Will it cannibalize other products, and if so, which ones? Will customers and employees accept this product as fitting in with the company's current image?
- What negative effects will the new product have on operations?
- Does the competition offer anything similar? How do the two products compare?
- Does your firm have the capability to develop and produce this item? What will it take in terms of time, expertise, facilities, labor, and budget?
- Will the new product require new equipment? If so, what kind and at what cost? Will the restaurant's labor needs be changed, and if so, in what way?

Prospective product ideas surviving the qualitative analysis should then be rated quantitatively, using the worksheet shown in Figure C.2.

Figure C.1
QUALITATIVE SCREENING WORKSHEET

1. Proposed new product_____

2. General description_____

3. Company objectives it will meet_____

4. Role it will play (circle one)   entree   side dish   new category product

5. Key strengths or opportunities_____

6. Key weaknesses or threats_____

7. Expected impact on sales (circle one)   increase traffic   increase frequency   trade up

     draw new customer group(s)   increase average check

8. Yearly sales goal_____   Profit-impact goal_____

9. Items it will cannibalize_____   To what degree_____

10. Target customers_____

11. Daypart(s) affected_____

12. Target price_____   Target portion size_____

13. Key ingredients_____

14. Estimated food costs_____

15. Expected production required_____

16. Current equipment required_____

17. New equipment required_____

18. Space required_____

19. Labor required_____

20. Additional employees required_____

21. Special training required_____

22. Negative effects on current production_____

23. Negative effects on staff_____

24. Similar competitive items_____

25. Likely competitive response_____

26. Key benefits_____

27. Key disadvantages_____

28. Required for development:

     a.   facilities_____

     b.   budget_____

     c.   personnel_____

     d.   special expertise_____

     e.   time_____

Figure C.2
QUANTITATIVE SCREENING WORKSHEET

CRITERIA	RATING (A)	WEIGHT (B)	TOTAL (A x B)
Image			
Menu approach			
Overall company goals			
Company strengths			
Company opportunities			
Desired role			
Level of quality			
Pricing			
Current customers			
Targeted customers			
Services			
Specialties			
Menu voids			
Day-part voids			
Production procedures			
Labor content			
Equipment			
Space availability			
Suppliers			
Developmental capabilities			
TOTAL			

Each new product idea is rated on a scale of 1 (low) to 5 (high) on each of the criteria. Then a weight of 1 to 5 is assigned to each criterion. The sum of these scores gives a final grand total for comparison with other proposed products.

In quantitative analysis, each new product idea is scored numerically according to criteria based on your company's priorities. Using a 5-point scale in which 1 is low and 5 is high works well. After the idea is rated according to the criteria, each criterion is ranked by importance or weight. Multiply each idea's rating by its weight, and then add the results to arrive at a total.

Using both forms of analysis—qualitative and quantitative—as a basis, ideas should be chosen for further development. You should pursue more than one product idea at a time, because some will inevitably run aground during development. The number of ideas selected should be realistic, however, so that your company's facilities are not unduly strained.

Step 2: Product Development. Product develoment involves many considerations and demands much testing. This step attempts to determine:

- Product configuration: size and shape.
- Product appearance: The aesthetic appeal is important!
- Consumer price: Will it sell?
- Packaging: Take-out and eat-in.
- Operational integration: Will the product fit easily into current operational procedures?
- Product supply and distribution: Will there be enough available product to meet various demand levels?

Step 3: Consumer Testing. If product development is successful, you should proceed to conduct focus-group consumer testing of the developed product before it is put into the market. This is an extremely critical step in the process since it provides an objective analysis of the product's attributes and potential viability. This testing often requires reformulation of the product—back to the drawing board, or rather, the kitchen.

Step 4: Test Marketing. You should select test markets that represent your entire system to validate the test, and testing should evaluate all the product development considerations mentioned in the second step. Media announcement of the product is an important part of this fourth step.

Step 5: Consumer Research. Research is the next phase and should determine customer acceptance levels under actual purchase conditions. The number will tell you a great deal about acceptance, but understanding the purchasers' perceptions and satisfaction level will provide reliable indicators of the product's longer-term viability in the real world.

Step 6: Analysis. At some point in time you must make a rollout decision based on the test marketing and research results. This requires analysis concentrating on incremental earnings, taking into account all costs associated with the product's introduction including equipment, labor training, advertising, media, POS materials, and so on.

Step 7: Rollout. The product is now expanded in an orderly fashion, geographically, sharing with your entire organization all relevant information and materials including:

- Product rationale
- Consumer attitudes
- Operational procedures
- Advertising and promotion support materials
- Test market data and results
- Training programs

If you fail to follow these basic product development guidelines, you risk failure and lose still another opportunity to succeed in the foodservice business.

APPENDIX C HIGHLIGHTS AND REVIEW

1) **Is your new product development program focused on products that integrate smoothly into your operation and into your customers' needs?**

2) **Are you in a position to effectively access consumer feedback about your new product alternatives from a variety of market segments? Locations?**

3) **Have you addressed possible and probable cannibalization of other menu items by your new product? If so, what will you do to maximize the opportunity on the upside?**

4) **Is your new product team totally familiar with foodservice operations, as well as marketing disciplines?**

Appendix D

20 Great Four-Walls Marketing Ideas

Four-Walls Marketing means stimulating business in your restaurant by exploiting opportunities right within your own four walls. The three areas targeted through Four-Walls Marketing are number of customers, frequency of current customers, and average guest check. There are many variations on these three themes. This appendix provides 20 examples.

Example 1. Increase the number of customers by offering a free buffet dinner during a happy hour period. This is a very popular tactic, used in the early evening, which draws people in for the food and encourages them to spend money on drinks.

Banana Max of Jupiter, Florida, takes the free buffet theme one step further. Customers put their business cards into a large glass jar, for a drawing to be held at another time. The winner of the drawing wins a party for 100 friends, complete with the free buffet—also open to the public—and four drinks for 25 cents each. The party is held between 6 and 9 P.M., but many of the 100 friends stay longer. Needless to say, everyone who drops their card into the jar is a "winner" and Banana Max is packed with people every night of the week.

Example 2. Beef up your customer count at lunch time with express lunches. This Four-Walls promotion guarantees service within a short amount of time—usually 5 to 15 minutes—or customers get their lunch free. Pizza Hut uses the express lunch to promote a 5-minute pizza. Instead of waiting for an average-sized pizza to cook—which many people don't have time for at lunch, especially those who get only a half-hour for lunch—Pizza Hut offers a tiny pizza for one person, guaranteed to be served in 5 minutes or be served free.

Example 3. Salad bars are another successful way to increase customer count, especially during lunch time. Salad bars allow customers to eat at their own pace, with variety and at a reasonable price. They've become so popular that many restaurants, from the Marriott to Wendy's, offer a salad bar to their customers. Another variation on the salad bar theme is offering brunch on Sundays at a special price.

Billy's of Decatur, Georgia, found that their Sundays were often slow. Their "Sunday Funday Brunch" offers three varieties of Eggs Benedict— regular, Georgia (country sausage is used instead of Canadian bacon), and seafood. The brunch has been successful. In fact, weekend brunch business, along with salad bars, has become very competitive throughout the country.

Example 4. Capitalize on your store's anniversary. Offer the prices that were instituted when your store opened.

Phil Smidt and Son of Hammond, Indiana, celebrated its anniversary by repeating its oldest menu and prices from the 1930s. The one-day celebration offered three entrees: lake perch, usually $10.00, was $1.25; frog legs, usually $10.95, were $1.50; and chicken, usually $5.50, was $1.25. Hundreds had to be turned away at the door, but 1,752 customers were served. It cost Phil Smidt between $10,000 and $15,000, but this loss was made up in three weeks with increased business due to all the publicity the anniversary created.

Mother's Day, St. Patrick's Day, Valentine's Day, and other special days offer still other ways to draw customers into your restaurant.

Example 5. A singles table is a great way to target the customer who is alone but doesn't want to eat alone. The Kansas City Marriott in Missouri reserves a special table seating 4 to 16 people. Seating, available for breakfast, lunch, and dinner, is voluntary, and is particularly popular with women. Marriott claims it makes money on the singles table because single people are not taking up tables meant for two or four. The singles table allows people to talk and get to know one another. It encourages the lone diner to come back. Best of all, it costs nothing.

Example 6. Another way to increase customer count is through birthday clubs, where customers fill out information about the date of their birthday, which you then keep on file. When a customer's birthday arrives, an invitation is sent, inviting the customer in for a free or discounted meal. Most people don't celebrate birthday dinners by themselves. Even if you give the customer a free meal, there is sure to be at least one guest who will buy dinner at the full price.

Birthday clubs are particularly popular with kids. Give them a free meal or a small gift. Either way, kids rarely redeem gifts by themselves.

They are sure to come in with Mom or Dad, or maybe even the rest of the family, who will all make purchases at the regular price.

Example 7. Get your employees to bring in new customers by staging an "employee incentive contest." Each employee—full- and part-time—gets a number of cards, say 50, to give to their friends, good for a special discount on an unlimited number of dinners or lunches within the promotional period. Each employee signs these cards, but cannot pass cards out in the restaurant. Also make sure the cards have an expiration date. Results can be tallied either by the number of cards redeemed, or by the entire gross sale. Either way, this promotion involves *all* your employees, and you get your advertising message distributed free.

Example 8. There are many ways to increase customer count during slow periods. One way is by offering an "Early Bird" special on meals served between 4 and 5 or 4:30 and 5:30 P.M., before your usual dinner crowd arrives.

You could give out "rain checks" to your customers on nice days, so that on stormy days, business will flow. These rain checks are discount coupons that can be redeemed only when it rains. When the rains hit, you'll be the only restaurant around not complaining of slow times.

To encourage dining over the holidays, the Four Seasons in New York City wishes its patrons happy holidays with a letter entitling them to one complimentary bottle of vintage champagne with dinner.

To combat slow Monday and Tuesday nights, the Chalet Restaurant of Roslyn, New York, offers selected wines at 50 percent off the regular price. Wines are those that are in large supply or not selling. Business has increased 30 percent, with many repeat customers trying wines they might not have otherwise tried.

Example 9. In-store activities can also stimulate business in your restaurant. There are many varieties of in-store activities. A few examples follow.

Ask a pro from a local tennis or racquetball club to give a talk on the fundamentals of the sport. The pro can answer questions on technique and equipment, and may distribute discount coupons for lessons at the club.

Engraving social security numbers or initials on CBs, portable radios, and tape recorders can help in the recovery of stolen items. Have one of your employees engrave this information on valuables for customers. This can increase customer traffic, while acting as an important community service.

Caricaturists draw attention wherever they work. Hire a talented high school or college student to draw caricatures of your customers. This is a good event to repeat, because those who attend your first caricature night will get the word around very quickly.

Example 10. Increase customer visits through frequency devices, designed to bring the customer back to your restaurant a specific number of times over a given period. If each of your customers visits your restaurant just one extra time each month, you would increase your volume by 50 percent. One excellent frequency device is the punch card. There are several types of punch cards. Some are based on a specific purchase amount, others on specific product purchases. Customers are given a card with a certain number of boxes, usually five or 10, depending on the length of the promotion. Each time the customer presents a card and makes the required purchase, the card is validated or punched. When all the boxes are completed, the card is then redeemed for a free product.

Punch card payout is excellent since many people will complete 50 to 75 percent of the required purchases, but will not keep the card long enough to redeem it for the free offer. Even if the card is redeemed, profit on the required purchases will more than offset the cost of the free offer. Hand out a five-box punch card, for example. Each time a customer makes a $3.00 purchase, the card is validated. After the card is completed, it is redeemed on the sixth visit for a free dinner-for-two. Cards should be distributed and validated for a four-week period, and then be redeemable during the following two-week period.

An innovative frequency device was implemented by C. I. Shenanigan's of Spokane, Washington. This company had a "passport to tasting" where customers were invited to try their liquor list of over 50 beers and imported liquors from over 20 countries. When the passport was completely validated, customers received special prizes. In its first nine-month trial, over 700 passports were given out; premium liquor sales were up 25 percent, and beer sales up 15 percent. Customers had to spend $150 to go through the list.

Example 11. Another standard frequency device is the bounceback coupon. Distributed over-the-counter, this invites your customers to return during a designated day or part of the day to take advantage of a special offer. This is a good way to use strong sales periods to help build weaker ones. For example, if you would like to build a weekday business, distribute a bounceback coupon on weekends, good only on the weekdays.

Coupons, in fact, are great business generators because they get customers involved in an offer, and they encourage them to react almost immediately, or within a very short period of time. Coupons can include "priceoff" discounts, "two-for-one" offers, and "buy one, get one free." Coupons reinforce your advertising message.

Example 12. Creating a demand for a product or service through successful advertising is usually not enough to increase sales in your restaurant. Four-Walls Marketing is needed to reinforce the advertising message, and is the prime function of point-of-purchase (POP), which is often referred to as point-of-sale (POS). Table tents are a great form of POP. Many people naturally pick up a table tent and study it carefully. Therefore, table tents make an excellent way to promote special menu items. Other standard types of POP materials include window displays, wall posters and hangers, countercards, counter displays, window and door stickers, floor displays, banners, and buttons promoting popular menu items.

Naturally, the type of POP materials required will depend on the type of promotion and, of course, budget. Creating POP materials can be expensive. One way to defray cost is to contact the manufacturer's representative of the products you're promoting. Many major suppliers or vendors have standard POP materials available to restaurant operators at little or no expense. For example, Coke has complete POP kits, including posters, countercards, and mobiles, showing Coke with various product combinations such as hamburgers, subs, or chicken.

Here are some tips on proper placement of POP:

1) Study the layout of your restaurant and determine optimum display points based on customer traffic and access. Behind the serving counter is an excellent place for POP.

2) Position POP materials where they can be readily seen by customers.

3) Avoid interference with actual serving areas. Try to unify all POP into one cohesive visual theme.

4) Regard POP material as a "silent sales rep" that can significantly affect sales of specific products and cause positive changes in the overall product mix over a period of time.

5) Rotate POP materials at least every other month in order to maintain customer interest. Moreover, it should dovetail with advertising.

Example 13. Pizza Hut uses placemats as very effective POP. They have to use placemats anyway, so why not use the space to advertise? While customers are waiting for food to arrive, they have something to look at. Pizza Hut uses one side of the placemat for games for kids. But the other side has become a great medium for advertising. And they are so effective, some radio and television stations have traded air time for exposure on the placemats. (This theme can also be carried over to tray liners for fast food operators.)

Example 14. When customers leave, they should always take something with them about your restaurant. This is called the "stuff-it" promotion, and it involves stuffing fliers into pickup order bags or doggie bags. Whether you offer a "buy one, get one free" or some kind of discount, fliers are an effective way for your customers to take your advertising message home with them.

Example 15. Smith and Wollensky's of New York City leaves pads of paper with its name on tables as reminders of where the customer business deals took place. Pads printed with "Notes Taken at Smith and Wollensky's" are left on every table. Each year 12,000 pads are printed, providing more than 300,000 memo sheets and reminders of the restaurant.

Example 16. Suggestive selling is a way to increase check amounts. This can be done by offering a side dish with an entree, such as when a customer orders a burger and the waitperson suggests french fries to go along with it. Waiters can also "trade up." Should a customer ask for a burger, the waiter might ask, "The deluxe burger?"

The Library of Myrtle Beach, South Carolina, is a restaurant that uses a "highest average check contest" to motivate its waitstaff to sell more. The contest runs for six months, with a prize of a trip for two awarded to the winner.

Example 17. Gift certificates are gifts that keeps on selling. McDonald's uses the gift certificate, worth about 50 cents, around Christmas. Besides the fact that a gift certificate brings in a customer who will probably spend more than the certificate is worth, a friend is sure to come along. Gift certificates are *prepayments* on food yet to be sold, and up to 20 percent of these gift certificates sold never even get redeemed!

Example 18. Zodiac signs are another great promotional device. People usually enjoy reading their horoscopes in the daily newspapers. Why not offer priceoff discounts each month for people born under the signs of that month?

Example 19. Unopened bottles of wine on the tables at Palazzino's Restaurant in Memphis, Tennessee, caused wine sales to increase 25 percent. Having the bottle on the table in view encourages customers to pick it up, examine it, and buy.

Another idea is to place empty wine glasses on your tables for lunch or dinner. Your employees may forget to ask if your customers want wine.

The empty wine glass can also serve as a reminder to the guest, who might otherwise not think of ordering wine.

Example 20. Grab publicity and increase overall sales by staging a contest for the millionth customer in your restaurant.

Scott's Seafood Embarcadero of San Francisco held such an event, where the millionth customer won a three-day trip to Carmel via a chauffeur-driven Rolls Royce. Business increased to a point where there was a three-hour wait with a turnover of nine times a day. On top of that, the owner had just opened another restaurant and the publicity from the promotion helped business there too.

The Fishmarket of Philadelphia uses buttons to promote popular menu items. A basket of buttons is placed by the front door. Most of the buttons don't mention the restaurant's name, but are so distinctive that most people recognize that they're from The Fishmarket.

The Sand Castle of Malibu, California, let customers know its beach-front restaurant was reopening after reconstruction due to a storm, by staging a sand castle competition, where only water and sand were allowed as materials. Due to its great success, the competition has become an annual event, with about 1,200 entries and four categories, in addition to promotional coverage by the media and newspapers.

The ideas for generating publicity are endless, but one thing is sure: Grabbing any opportunity for publicity is a profitable Four-Walls Marketing tactic.

Appendix E

Success Through Franchising

There is another way to success in foodservice beyond the marketing methodologies already described—another gigantic step you can take that will change the whole outlook and magnitude of your operations. Some of you have already taken that step, for better or worse. Others may have contemplated this important move but backed away because of poor or inadequate advice. Perhaps you should be considering this momentous change in business direction but haven't yet grasped its potential.

That important step is franchising, and no matter which of the foregoing categories best describes your situation, the information in this chapter should be of great value.

Despite its attractions, of course, franchising may not be for everybody. That's why you should complete the franchising feasibility audit pictured in Figure E.1.

Suppose that your franchising feasibility audit results have proven positive, that the rabbit has died. What you have to realize immediately is that if you decide to franchise, you will give birth to a completely new business: selling and supporting franchises.

There are some things you should be prepared to take into account and to act on before you go into this challenging, but potentially superprofitable new business.

Remember that you are not just selling the franchisee a new business, but a new lifestyle that combines entrepreneurial challenge, new independence, new wealth, new responsibilities, and some possibly surprising new demands.

The franchisee, as an assured return on investment, will expect from you a clear blueprint, with all the bugs worked out, that can be followed without having to call you every day for trouble-shooting. At the same

Figure E.1
FRANCHISING FEASIBILITY AUDIT

(Mark your position on the scale; place your scores in the boxes on the right.)

1. Identify the five key success factors in the foodservice industry; then, score your restaurant relative to the industry.

Key success factor _____   ❏

-10 _____ +10

| | | |
| -5 | 0 | +5 |

Key success factor _____   ❏

-10 _____ +10

| | | |
| -5 | 0 | +5 |

Key success factor _____   ❏

-10 _____ +10

| | | |
| -5 | 0 | +5 |

Key success factor _____   ❏

-10 _____ +10

| | | |
| -5 | 0 | +5 |

Key success factor _____   ❏

-10 _____ +10

| | | |
| -5 | 0 | +5 |

2. List the top five business risks in your industry; then, score your own company relative to the foodservice industry.

Business Risk _____

-10 _____ +10
                   -5   0   +5

Business Risk _____

-10 _____ +10
                   -5   0   +5

Business Risk _____

-10 _____ +10
                   -5   0   +5

Business Risk _____

-10 _____ +10
                   -5   0   +5

Business Risk _____

-10 _____ +10
                   -5   0   +5

3. Estimate the financial resources available up front for development of your new business of franchising.

$0	$50K	$75K	$100K	$150K
-200	-100	0	+100	+200

Figure E.1 (*continued*)

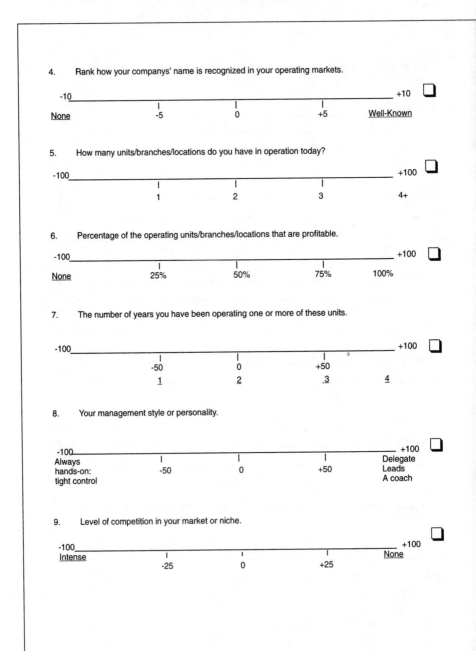

4. Rank how your companys' name is recognized in your operating markets.

-10 _____ +10 ☐
None   -5   0   +5   Well-Known

5. How many units/branches/locations do you have in operation today?

-100 _____ +100 ☐
              1   2   3   4+

6. Percentage of the operating units/branches/locations that are profitable.

-100 _____ +100 ☐
None   25%   50%   75%   100%

7. The number of years you have been operating one or more of these units.

-100 _____ +100 ☐
             -50   0   +50
              1   2   3   4

8. Your management style or personality.

-100 _____ +100 ☐
Always   -50   0   +50   Delegate
hands-on: Leads
tight control   A coach

9. Level of competition in your market or niche.

-100 _____ +100 ☐
Intense   None
             -25   0   +25

Figure E.1 (*continued*)

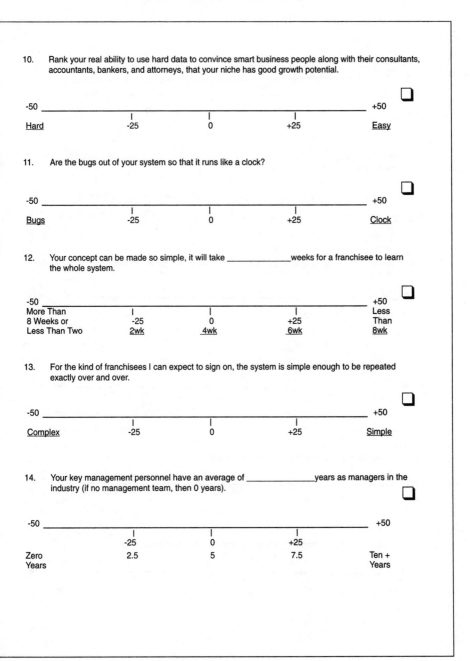

10. Rank your real ability to use hard data to convince smart business people along with their consultants, accountants, bankers, and attorneys, that your niche has good growth potential.

-50 _____ +50
Hard   -25   0   +25   Easy

11. Are the bugs out of your system so that it runs like a clock?

-50 _____ +50
Bugs   -25   0   +25   Clock

12. Your concept can be made so simple, it will take _____weeks for a franchisee to learn the whole system.

-50 _____ +50
More Than   -25   0   +25   Less
8 Weeks or   Than
Less Than Two   2wk   4wk   6wk   8wk

13. For the kind of franchisees I can expect to sign on, the system is simple enough to be repeated exactly over and over.

-50 _____ +50
Complex   -25   0   +25   Simple

14. Your key management personnel have an average of _____years as managers in the industry (if no management team, then 0 years).

-50 _____ +50
                    -25   0   +25
Zero   2.5   5   7.5   Ten +
Years   Years

Figure E.1 (*continued*)

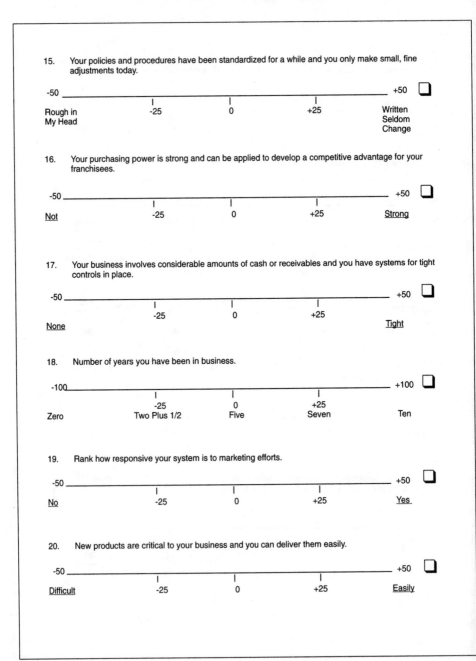

15. Your policies and procedures have been standardized for a while and you only make small, fine adjustments today.

-50 ——————————————————————— +50 ☐
Rough in   -25   0   +25   Written
My Head   Seldom
                                                                     Change

16. Your purchasing power is strong and can be applied to develop a competitive advantage for your franchisees.

-50 ——————————————————————— +50 ☐
Not   -25   0   +25   Strong

17. Your business involves considerable amounts of cash or receivables and you have systems for tight controls in place.

-50 ——————————————————————— +50 ☐
None   -25   0   +25   Tight

18. Number of years you have been in business.

-100 ——————————————————————— +100 ☐
Zero   -25   0   +25   Ten
                  Two Plus 1/2   Five   Seven

19. Rank how responsive your system is to marketing efforts.

-50 ——————————————————————— +50 ☐
No   -25   0   +25   Yes

20. New products are critical to your business and you can deliver them easily.

-50 ——————————————————————— +50 ☐
Difficult   -25   0   +25   Easily

Figure E.1 (*continued*)

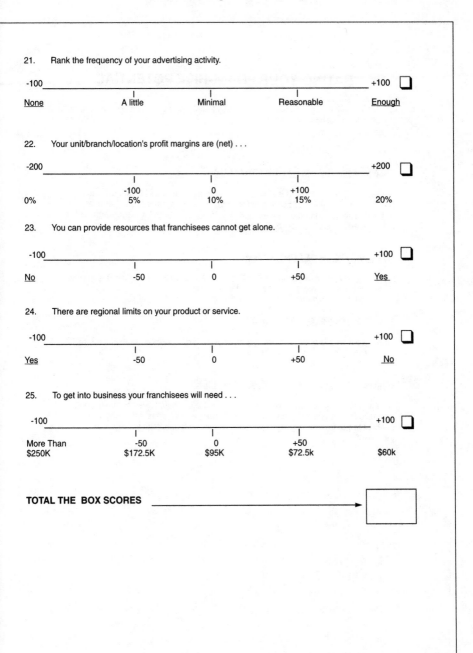

21. Rank the frequency of your advertising activity.

-100   +100 ☐

None   A little   Minimal   Reasonable   Enough

22. Your unit/branch/location's profit margins are (net) . . .

-200   +200 ☐

      -100   0   +100

0%   5%   10%   15%   20%

23. You can provide resources that franchisees cannot get alone.

-100   +100 ☐

No   -50   0   +50   Yes

24. There are regional limits on your product or service.

-100   +100 ☐

Yes   -50   0   +50   No

25. To get into business your franchisees will need . . .

-100   +100 ☐

More Than   -50   0   +50
$250K $172.5K $95K $72.5k $60k

TOTAL THE BOX SCORES   ⟶ ☐

Figure E.1 (*continued*)

RATING YOUR FRANCHISE POTENTIAL

When you have completed your "Franchising Feasibility Audit," compare your total score to the following rankings:

-1960 to -960: RETHINK YOUR STRATEGY

You have not demonstrated that you have a concept with franchising potential. Your business may in fact be on solid footing, but there are hurdles to get over first. If you score high on questions 3, 8, 12, 18, and 25, adopt a longer-term view and address the other issues in your plans.

-955 to 0: YOU'RE GETTING WARM

If you scored high in questions 3, 8, 12, 18 and 25, as well as 5, 6, and 9, you need more fine tuning before you can attempt to franchise.

0 to +960: YOU'RE ON YOUR WAY

Seek help if time is your problem. If you received high scores on questions 3, 8, 12, 18, and 25, the rest is all downhill.

+960 to +1960: JUST HANG ON FOR THE RIDE

With good scores on questions 3, 8, 12, 18, and 25, you just need to codify your business format and systems, build in a few bells and whistles, and bring your concept to the franchising market . . . you are ready to package your business for sale!

272

Figure E.1 (*continued*)

Figure E.2
FRANCHISING "VALUE PAK" TIMELINE

FOUR WEEK PERIODS

FRANCHISE COMPONENT	1	2	3	4	5	6	7	8	9	10	11	12	13
Corporate Marketing Plan	----90 Days---												
Corporate Business Plan			----90 Days---										
Marketing Plan for Franchise Sales	---45 Days--												
Operations Planning and Management Guide													
Franchise Sales and Compliance Program				--60 Days									
Preopening, Opening, and Grand Opening Guide				--60 Days									
Trade Area Marketing Guide				--60 Days									
Training and Human Resources Guide	----------150 Days------												
Legal Materials (Gunster, Yoakley, et al.)		--60 Days											
(New Proposal) Long-Term Retainer						------------------------------------							
START DATE													
STOP DATE													
PAYMENT ALLOCATION													
PAYMENT DAY													

time, you must be ready to service the franchisee when necessary, to provide a reliable safety net, to meet unanticipated market shifts. As part of your franchise sale package you'll want to make it very clear that you've worked out all foreseeable contingencies and can offer a system for handling the unforeseen.

You will also have to convince your franchising prospects that your prototype operations are sound and transferrable, that your support organization stands ready to meet franchising industry standards and expectations, and that you've met legal requirements across the board.

The remaining pages of this appendix presents a "Value Pak" that you can use as the basis for entering the franchise business. The timeline in Figure E.2 will help you put the franchise package into place. Then, each item in the "Value Pak" is briefly described, and the description is complemented by a listing of the item key components.

CORPORATE MARKETING PLAN

This strategic document incorporates your key success factors from the past along with broad-vision expansion and describes the impact franchising has on your business. It will serve as your guide for retaining your niche, selling franchises, and managing growth. It represents the first "go"/"no go" determination point in the franchising decision.

A. Researching and Understanding the Market
    1. Set objectives and define methodology
    2. Source and apply secondary research
    3. Source and apply primary research
    4. Set up procedure and calculate market(s) potential
    5. Sales/share analysis

B. Alternative Development and Selection
    1. Establish corporate mission reflecting franchising
    2. Set goals, scope, objectives
    3. Conduct situation analysis
    4. Generate alternative marketing strategies
    5. Establish profile of target consumers
    6. Assess impact of social/demo trends
    7. Identify key factors driving current operation's sales
    8. Set up formal operation/franchise analysis and approval criteria
    9. Formulate detailed programs to build sales for company/franchise

C. Product Planning and Development
    1. Set objectives by consumer segment and product category
    2. Organize for analysis
    3. Apply research findings
    4. Establish corporate positioning and image for consumers and franchise sales
    5. Formalize approach

6. Find and appraise new products
7. Write up findings

D. Distribution Channels for Expanded Products/Geographic Markets
1. Set functions and objectives
2. Evaluate alternatives
3. Select specific channel
4. Highlight key areas of concern
5. Procedures to work with channels/franchisees
6. Administrative issues
7. Impact on management/personnel requirements
8. Impact on franchisee financial resources
9. Sales training of franchisee field support force
10. Rough out sales promotion and advertising requirements
11. Impact on channels at various sales levels
12. Impact on franchisees at various sales levels

E. Assessment of Supply
1. Raw materials
2. Manufacturing
3. Other

F. Pricing
1. Rationalize current strategy and impact
2. Set objectives
3. Clarify elements critical to pricing development
4. Identify and assess external influencing factors
5. Incorporate research
6. Assess relationships
7. Establish strategy
8. Set price recommendations
9. Develop alternative price procedures

G. Summary and Direction for Marketing
1. Overall cost leadership
2. Differentiation
3. Focus

H. Advertising
1. Establish procedures for setting objectives
2. Determine advertising strategy
3. Determine the message
4. Evaluate media options
5. Develop the advertising budget
6. Formalize the department

    7. Select advertising services supplier
    8. Establish relationship with service suppliers
    9. Coordinate advertising/promotional events
  10. Implementation/execution procedures
  11. Establish program/promotion criteria and formats
  12. Establish techniques to track
  13. Establish techniques to evaluate tracking
  14. Consumer awareness evaluation
  15. Recall testing
  16. Management reporting format and policy

I. Public Relations
    1. Set objectives
    2. Assign management responsibility
    3. Develop PR execution plan
    4. Finalize activities/events
    5. Execution
    6. Prepare news releases and articles
    7. Place company speakers
    8. Write up plan

J. Develop Grand Opening Program
    1. Establish objectives
    2. Define components
    3. Trade area profile
    4. Formalize preopening setup steps
    5. Establish postopening shakedown period
    6. Public relations
    7. Weekly checklists
    8. Develop creative materials
    9. Develop franchisee order forms

K. Determine Marketing Support Materials
    1. Sustaining
    2. Periodic
    3. Merchandising/displays
    4. Execution
    5. Promotions

CORPORATE BUSINESS PLAN

Rapid market expansion and penetration via franchising totally change the form and structure of your business You need to explore changes, assess impact, make decisions, and produce a five-year business plan to direct your efforts. This represents the second "go"/"no go" decision point in the franchising determination.

Business Planning Components

A. Where the Company Is Today
B. Key Factors and Impact/Implication
C. Key Industry Success Factors
D. Key Strengths and Needs
E. Impact on Form of Doing Business Using Franchising
F. Product Distribution Structures
G. Impact on Manufacturing and Channels
H. Financing for Franchising
I. Pricing: Fees, Royalties, Other
J. Establishing Initial Franchisee Investment
K. Assessment of Issues Found
L. Summarize for Inclusion into Business Plan

Business Planning Components

(The specific road map for your franchising activities and your premiere selling material)

A. History of Company
B. Business Summary
C. Outlet/Facility Plan
D. Operating and Personnel Plan
E. Products and Services
F. Marketing and Sales
G. Competition
H. Research and Development
I. Management
J. Funds and Terms Required
K. Financial Reports and Explanations to Meet FTC/UFOC Requirements
L. Capitalization: Equity
M. Capitalization: Debt

Marketing Plan for Franchise Sales

A.   Researching the Markets for Franchising

B.   Alternative Development and Selection

C.   Franchise Planning and Development

D.   Pricing the Product

E.   Support Services to Execute Programs

F.   Management of Fees

G.   Advertising/Recruitment of Franchisees

H.   Public Relations

I.   Marketing Plan Support Materials

OPERATIONS PLANNING AND MANAGEMENT GUIDE

Each detail of your successful business behaviors is refined into a blueprint that can be used by franchisees to learn from your behavior and emulate it.

A.   Introduction to Franchisees/Company Operations
    1.   Letter from President
        a.   Missions and commitments
        b.   Business philosophy/values
        c.   Establish strategic business unit
        d.   Commitment to franchise agreement
        e.   Responsibilities of company and franchisees to each other
        f.   Establish strategies
            (1)   Institutional
            (2)   Business
            (3)   Corporate
        g.   Corporate history
        h.   How to use the manual
        i.   The franchise agreement and you
        j.   Company organization by function
        k.   Managing—your primary function

B. Customer Service
   1. The market
   2. In-store/shop/on-territory sales
C. Products and General Rules/Procedures for Operating
D. Daily Functions
E. Management Accounting Guidelines
F. On-Site Inspection by Franchisor
G. Rules, Regulations, Policies for Day-to-Day Store Operations and Employees
H. Forms, Computer Software, Reporting System

FRANCHISE SALES AND COMPLIANCE PROGRAM

A. Planning and Compliance
   1. Characteristics of target franchisee profile
   2. Detailed sales positioning and programs
   3. Advertising/recruitment for franchisees in compliance with regulatory bodies
   4. Federal and state regulation administration
   5. Review of compliance
   6. Franchise policy/executive committee (FPC/FEC)
   7. Required record keeping
B. Generating Leads
   1. Seminar program
   2. Advertising
   3. Brochures
   4. Marketing strategy
   5. Corporate strategy
   6. Product strategy
   7. Operations and accounting
   8. Training
   9. Real estate and construction
   10. Application process/administration
C. Followup on Leads
   1. Initial contact procedures
   2. Sales objectives
   3. Techniques

D. Selling and Compliance
    1. Evaluating corporate responsibility
    2. Control of selling personnel
    3. Background checks
    4. State registrations
    5. Screening applicants

PREOPENING, OPENING, AND GRAND OPENING GUIDE

This guide takes your franchisees through the detailed steps from franchise signing until six months after opening, with dates set so they don't miss even the smallest detail while setting up your business format.

A. Introduction
    1. Previous plans
    2. UFOC requirements
    3. Franchise sales promises
    4. Training
B. Develop Preopening Checklist (CPM with expanded text)
    1. Lead time for each function
    2. Company personnel on site
C. Opening Through First 45 Days
    1. In location/market activities
    2. Outreach activities
    3. Blending into corporate plans
D. Six Months after Opening
    1. Implementing master marketing plan
    2. Evaluating and adjusting
    3. Develop first operation-level marketing plan

TRADE AREA MARKETING GUIDE

This step-by-step handbook guides your franchisee through sales-building activities in the local community while supporting your image and positioning.

A. Researching the Trade Area
    1. Profile from corporate plans
    2. Set objectives
    3. Source consumer data

B. Alternative Development and Selection
    1. Generate alternative strategies
    2. Evaluate competition
    3. Rationalize strategy

C. Formulate Detailed Programs to Build Business
    1. Source corporate programs
    2. Determine types of activities

D. Budgeting at the Store Level
    1. Set time line, provide forms
    2. Review alternatives
    3. Clarify revenue stream, charges, and flow through
    4. Set in controls

E. Materials Provided by Company or Advertising Cooperative: Inventory In-Store
    1. Slicks, telemarketing, tapes, etc. from pool
    2. Ordering forms
    3. Tracking forms
    4. Activity calendars
    5. Procedures for using media
    6. Business analysis forms
    7. Use guidelines
    8. Merchandising/sales materials

F. Catalogue and Distribution
    1. Set up guidelines
    2. Ordering instructions
    3. Corporate procedures
        a. Inventory/reorder system
        b. Administration
    4. Support
    5. Procedures

TRAINING AND HUMAN RESOURCES GUIDE

This guide covers all aspects of personnel management and the transfer of skills that support a successful novice franchisee.

Training

A. Policy Guideline Development
   1. Reference all manuals
   2. Reference all legal documents
   3. Establish costs and who pays
   4. Set locations, dates, accommodations
   5. Establish components/elements of training and objectives
   6. Set training standards and measures
B. Training Steps
   1. Explanation
   2. Demonstration
   3. Performance
   4. Followup
C. Techniques and Elements
   1. Learner-controlled instruction
   2. Curriculum
   3. Materials
   4. Classroom techniques
   5. Coordination of changes

Human Resources

A. Set Objectives
   1. Policy in all areas
   2. Job content/analysis/functions
   3. Job descriptions
      a. Responsibilities
      b. Equipment operations
B. The Employment Process: Recruiting
   1. Application administration
   2. Reference authorizations
   3. Ad slicks
   4. Manager's guide to recruiting, interviewing, orienting, training
C. Employee Training Handbook
   1. Task sheets
   2. Orientation to job
   3. New hire training schedule
   4. Functional/position description and guide
   5. Ongoing job schedules

D.   Salary Administration
1.   Introduction and policy
2.   Responsibilities
3.   Forms administration
4.   Job evaluation
5.   Program administration
6.   Time sheets, record keeping, and payment
7.   Legal issues
8.   Salary schedule and guidelines
9.   Raises and promotions

E.   Managing Human Performance
1.   Introduction and policy
2.   Performance objectives and expectations
3.   Observing and documenting performance
4.   Coaching for improved performance
5.   Review of overall performance
6.   On-the-job planning
7.   Franchisee training program

F.   Taking Effective Disciplinary Action
1.   General guidelines
2.   Disciplinary and termination report
3.   Probation
4.   Termination
5.   Resignation
6.   Franchisee training program
7.   Forms administration

Appendix F

Off-Premise Group Sales: On Target for Profits

Convenience has become a key factor in food consumption choices. Today's lifestyles often demand fast, good-tasting food available by delivery or customer pickup. By complementing your food with an easy ordering procedure and reliable delivery you can attract an increased share of off-premise consumers needing large-quantity orders.

The advantages of developing an off-premise group sales program are:

- An increase in your current customer base
- Building awareness of your restaurant
- More productive utilization of your staff
- The possibility of attracting consumers to your restaurant after experiencing your product at a group event

The opportunities for outside group sales abound. Operating an off-premise program, however, requires pacing, commitment, dedication, and a plan. By starting small, setting goals, and following an effective, well-charted course of action, your outside group business can grow steadily over time.

Start as soon as possible, but start slowly and work at your own pace, building your confidence and your expertise as you grow. Begin with the development of delivery service and group sales using your current, unheated menu items. Then you can build a catering and home delivery operation offering these services for both private and public events.

OFF-PREMISE OPPORTUNITIES

Group sales generally means offering your services to a party or special event through pickup or delivery of established minimum orders. Group events include such things as home parties, office events, school events, social events, church events, and civic and fraternal events. Look at the possibilities. Business firms alone host a number of events during the year, such as retirement parties, annual meetings, ground-breaking ceremonies, grand openings, anniversary celebrations, and holiday office caterings.

The following types of locations often require foodservice capability beyond the scope of on-premise facilities:

- Offices/Stores
- Plants
- Military bases
- Hospitals
- Convention centers
- Motels
- Nursing homes
- Schools

HOW TO BEGIN

Using a map, determine the location of potential delivery and pickup opportunities, designating a larger area for pickup than for delivery. Now, create a list of target places within these areas. (Another option is to deliver anywhere and simply add delivery costs to the price.)

The next step is to uncover any problems, statutes, or ordinances that would prevent you from pursuing a location or event on your list. For example, local municipalities may have a licensing requirement for transporting goods on public property. Local laws may dictate that when you prepare food for sale outside of your restaurant, you need an additional health permit.

Proper insurance on any vehicle used in delivery is necessary, and anyone driving the vehicle must also be covered. Dealing with large groups means extra precautions regarding safety as well as certainty that you are covered by public liability and products liability insurance. "All risk" insurance is normally an additional coverage to your current insurance. So, consult your insurance company or agent for proper advice.

DELIVERY AND PICKUP HOURS

When arranging delivery and pickup hours you must schedule product preparation times to ensure freshness. Yet you should also avoid disrupting normal hourly and daily traffic peaks to maintain current customer satisfaction with product and service.

STAFFING

Naturally, it is important to have a professional, well-trained staff to represent your restaurant in selling the service, taking orders, preparing, and delivering your product. As this area of your business grows, it may be necessary to select specific staffers to handle off-premise group sales or even to hire an additional person. That person should enjoy dealing with the public and be able to sell persuasively. As the delivery component of group sales grows, you should consult with appropriate federal agencies to review the laws and regulations applicable to the employment-related aspects of the program, such as wage and hour regulations, record keeping, and reporting requirements and state employment laws.

PRICING SUGGESTIONS

There are several ways to charge for your services, and you can negotiate with each client to fit the particular occasion. While you should offer a special rate on group orders, that rate can take several forms. A special, for example, could take the form of free delivery with orders of a minimum dollar amount, say $25 within a specified area. An idea for pickup orders would be to take 10 percent off the regular price—again for orders of $25 or more. Remember to consider your competition when setting your pricing structure. A few phone calls will give you this information. Allow your delivery person to keep any tips.

QUALITY ASSURANCE AND DISTRIBUTION

To keep your food in good condition, you must maintain an adequate temperature. This may require refrigeration in transit. Also, when transporting food, remember to use care when stacking in order to avoid damaging it. A temperature-controlled truck might facilitate transit when your volume warrants it.

ADMINISTRATION AND ORDER TAKING

Very large group orders or regular off-premise group orders may require a contract. Contracts can be tailored to suit the needs of a particular client or event. Once you've worked out the details of your program, you'll want to develop a group order insert for your menu. This should include the following information:

- Delivery hours and days
- Delivery range (i.e., number of miles from your restaurant you can deliver)
- Items available for delivery
- Prices or discounts available
- Number to call and the name of the person to speak with

This menu should be typeset, attractive, neat, and easy to read. Avoid clutter. Post a group order menu insert near your phone to help employees answer phone inquiries.

You'll also need an order form to maintain organization. It's best to order carbonless three-part forms for restaurant and customer copies. Two copies should go with the order and must be signed by the customer. The third is the control copy, which is kept in the restaurant. Keep a supply of forms near the phone and behind the counter for easy access. Staff should be thoroughly familiarized with the forms, phone procedures, and means of expediting the order. A sample form is shown in Figure F.1.

When taking an order, remind your customer of your delivery range and minimum order requirements. *Always* reread the order to the customer exactly as it was written to avoid any errors. Discuss the form of payment before pickup delivery and inform the customer if you accept cash only. Your delivery person should carry only enough cash to make

Figure F.1
GROUP SALES ORDER FORM

INSTRUCTIONS

CARBONLESS THREE-PART FORM

Top Copy

Middle Copy `}` Both go out. One comes back to match with bottom copy.

Bottom Copy   Control copy in restaurant.

NAME: _____ TIME CALLED: _____

ADDRESS: _____ PHONE: _____

_____ DATE: _____

ORDER: _____

_____

AMOUNT: _____ FORM OF PAYMENT: _____

AMOUNT TENDERED: _____ CHANGE: _____

COMMENTS: _____

_____

_____

CUSTOMER SIGNATURE: _____

change. Always get the customer's phone number in case a problem arises. Tell the customer when to expect delivery (i.e., within the hour); then *be sure* the delivery is on time. Save names and addresses and develop a mailing list.

If you don't already have one, this may be a good time to set up a charge card system in your restaurant to offer added convenience to your group customers. To make it worth your while, you may want to require a minimum purchase for credit card orders.

SELLING

Make initial contact with targeted businesses or organizations to set up meetings with those in charge of ordering for special events. Also, offer your services to local social or civic clubs and associations. Don't forget that newspapers, radio, local publications, and the Yellow Pages can help you reach potential customers.

Load several trays with samples of your products, parade them through the business district at lunch time, and let the public do some sampling. Be sure to provide a handout explaining the program to those receiving samples.

Refer to your target audience list. Consider a direct mail letter or the distribution of fliers/menus with inserts to office buildings. You can simply announce the availability of your group order program, or you may want to appeal to your customers by offering first-time incentives.

Your staff can be your best selling tool. Hold a staff meeting to explain the details of your group order program. Each crew member, regardless of whether they will deliver product or not, should be well informed about your group order service. Over the phone or behind the counter, they should be able to answer intelligently all questions regarding pricing, minimum orders, delivery range, and delivery hours. An internal sales incentive program could help as well. Encourage staff members to use suggestive selling techniques to inform customers about your service and to use menu inserts or fliers as handouts.

If you are interested in concentrating on local business, contact receptionists or secretaries, as they are the ones most likely to place orders. Stop by their offices and leave a menu with a group order insert. Offer "trial" incentives, such as a bonus serving or a dollar-off special. Consider offering an additional incentive for pickup.

MAKING A SALES CALL FOR LARGE GROUP ORDERS

Once you have created interest and awareness through your marketing efforts and have gotten an initial appointment, you may want to go over these points before your meeting:

- Bring samples to the meeting
- Offer special first time prices
- Express willingness to tailor your service
- Offer to make a presentation that fits the prospect's image or event theme

Figure F.2
GROUP SALES
CONTRACT AND AGREEMENT

Organization _____   Date _____

Person in Charge _____   Set for # _____

Phone _____   Guarantee _____

Address _____   Deposit 20% _____
_____   Based on Guarantee:
                                                     Method of Payment:
                                                     Cash _____
Time _____   Credit _____

TYPE OF FUNCTION _____

Special Arrangements or Provisions _____
_____
_____

MENU _____
_____
_____   Price per person _____

Payment shall be made immediately following the function unless credit has been established. Any accounts that have been extended credit are to be paid within 10 days* of the function.

A 20 percent (20%) deposit* is required at time of confirmation. The deposit will be refunded if guest cancels seven days* prior to the confirmed date. The deposit is nonrefundable if guest cancels less than seven days* prior to the confirmed date.

If the listed arrangements meet with your approval, please sign this agreement.

SIGNATURE _____   TOTAL _____

                        DATE OF   LESS
TITLE _____ CONFIRMATION _____   DEPOSIT _____

ABC RESTAURANT   (Enter at time of confirmation)

BY _____   BALANCE DUE _____

DATE _____

*INSERT YOUR TERMS

After the interview, quickly send a proposal you feel will meet the customer's needs. Then follow up immediately with a phone call. Once you've developed a mutually acceptable proposal, prepare a contract for your new customer. Figure F.2 is a sample group sales contract and agreement.

PACKAGING OFF-PREMISE SALES

Using your creativity to coordinate your packaging with holidays and special events will enhance your delivery service. This may include the use of colorful ribbons or balloons for special occasions. A unique party package for birthday parties, office parties, or going-away parties may be incorporated into your group sales service as well. If boxes are used, they should show your restaurant's name and the name of the person selected to conduct your group sales merchandising activities.

Off-premise group sales present you with yet another opportunity to succeed in the foodservice group. The steps and procedures outlined in the following program will help you to enlarge that opportunity.

OFF-PREMISE GROUP SALES PROGRAM

Prepared by:

Date:

Program	Sales Calls to Businesses/Organizations for Off-Premise Group Sales
Program Objective	Sell ABC menu items through group sales by individual sales calls.
Explanation	Off-premise group sales to organizations and businesses in your area can generate significant sales. This can result when an organized program for selling, preparing, pickup, and delivery is in effect. Start out by selecting the names of good prospects in your trading area for off-premise group sales. Contact the owners and managers of these facilities by phone, asking for an appointment to explain the program. At the time of your visit, show them photographs and offer samples of the kind of food items you could provide to them on a regular basis. You should be close to receiving an order by this time, but if you don't have one, allow several days to go by and then call your contact again for a decision. You should continue the program by contacting several businesses or groups per week to generate a continuing off-premise group sales program.
Materials	Solicitation letter Photos of menu items

Timetable/Implementation

Date	Activity
Seven weeks prior	Send solicitation letter
Six weeks prior	Arrange appointments
Five weeks prior	Meet with managers to show photos and provide samples of your menu items
Three weeks prior	Make followup phone calls
Two weeks prior	Obtain orders
One week prior	Inform staff, prepare menu items
Start program	Make deliveries

SAMPLE LETTER

Date:

Address:

Dear Mr./Mrs. _____:

We are the ABC Restaurant at 123 Datura Street, and want you to know that we are a neighbor of yours and are offering a special program to you.

As you may know, the ABC specializes in sandwiches and cakes and pies that have won extraordinary acceptance by our community.

The terrific response we have experienced from our consumers has prompted us to make our menu items available to you in quantities for group gatherings for special events or on a regular basis at special prices.

The program we are offering to you permits you to serve our high quality, tasty food items at your own facility or one that you designate. We prepare and deliver the product. You serve the product. It is that simple.

Please call me at ___(phone)___ in order to arrange an appointment for you to see our variety and taste our product. You'll be glad you did.

Sincerely,

Jim Smith

Program	Group Sales Through Restaurant Party
Program Objective	Encourage decision makers to see and taste sandwiches, dessert, and other items that are available to serve at their events or functions.
Explanation	Send invitations for "Sandwich, Cake, and Pie Sampling" party to local business owners and managers for a "By Invitation Only" party to be held at the ABC Restaurant. (Allow them to bring husband, wife, or guest if they so desire.)

Decorate for occasion. Fresh flowers and tablecloths add to the festivity of the evening. (Consider renting additional tables and chairs, if necessary.)

There should be a hostess at the door to give out name tags and greet everyone and servers to cut and serve the sandwiches, cakes, and pies. Remember that presentation is critical.

Make sure you have sign-up sheets or forms to provide the opportunity for them to sign up right away (preferably) or to take with them. If they take them with them, be sure to follow up by phone in a couple of days to thank them for attending and ask for an order.

The invitation should carry an RSVP to help you plan your party.

Materials	Invitations
	Flowers
	Name tags
	Sign-up sheets/forms
	Flier explaining program

Timetable/Implementation

Date	Activity
Four weeks prior	Contact local restaurateurs and discuss party
Three weeks prior	Print up invitations and RSVPs and sign-up sheets, flier explanation programs
Two weeks prior	Pick up name tags, etc., and order additional chairs/tables for party
One week prior	Pick up invitations and prepare for mailing
	Hold staff meeting and discuss responsibilities and operational execution
	Send out invitations
Evening before party	Decorate and set up the restaurant
Party day	Make staff assignments
	Contact restaurateurs as follow up
	Evaluate results

Appendix G

You Don't Have to Be Number One to Be Number One: Avoiding the Positioning Pitfall

When you attempt to develop a positioning statement, there is a great temptation to think that you should be positioned as number one in some major category or geographical area. That's not too surprising, given the general American obsession with being number one. That obsession is expressed every weekend during football season, when wide receivers and running backs hold up their index fingers after scoring a touchdown.

But you don't have to be number one to be number one.

What is number one in the restaurant business? Some people think being the biggest makes a firm number one. Others think that being the most profitable makes them number one. Actually, one company is not necessarily better because it is bigger, any more than an elephant is better because it is bigger than a dog. According to Peter Drucker, a business must be the right size for its market, its economy, and its technology—and the right size is whatever produces the optimal yield from your firm's resources.

You can top those formidable competitors, but you don't do it everywhere, and not all at once. Military strategists know that it is best if *you* pick the time and place for a battle. And if you're facing a force larger than your own, or one that is better equipped, you don't fix bayonets and attack head-to-head. You're far better off if you fight only part of the

enemy force, or if you can surprise the enemy by attacking at an unex-
pected time or place or in a surprising manner. So, you don't have to battle
giants head-to-head. That big adversary may be so busy defending an
entire position that he won't lower himself to a skirmish over a tiny part
of his domain. So you can dominate—even if it is only a relatively small
territory you dominate. In that territory, you can be number one. In
marketing circles, this approach is sometimes called "niche marketing,"
so find a niche for your operation—a niche in which it is simply better
than anyone else's—and exploit that position.

Perhaps you've already done this so you know that this kind of growth
comes from exploiting opportunity, and that it requires concentration.
The greatest mistake in a growth strategy, and the most common one, is
to try to grow in too many areas. Again, according to Drucker, a growth
strategy has to think through the targets of opportunity—that is, the
areas in which your strengths are most likely to produce extraordinary
results.

Where can you look for your niche? There are four areas in which you
can differentiate yourself from your competition. And, remember, the
greater the differentiation, the greater your chances for success. (Of course,
that differentiation must be meaningful, not just some more me-too
ideas.)

First, you pick out a certain kind of consumer and make that consumer
someone to whom your name sets off cannons and whistles and music.
The second area has to do with producing a "special kind of experience"
consumers get when they visit your restaurant. The third niche has to do
with penetration of new units, filling in the gaps on an accelerated basis
and cultivating much stronger working relationships with your operators/
managers so that they keep you informed about new opportunities.

The fourth niche is price or added value. While it is nice to discount
heavily and undersell the competition, no one is always going to have the
lowest price or best deal all the time. In fact, it is those companies that
have built a niche for their names by outperforming the competition that
are consistently successful in adding real value.

Let's elaborate on these four elements in niche marketing.

You can pick out a certain kind of consumer and make that consumer a
fanatic. As an example, take the coffee business, dominated by brands like
Maxwell House and Folgers. Their distribution is incredible, and their
advertising budgets look like the gross national product. Nevertheless,
there is a group of competitors who have built very healthy and profitable
businesses in the coffee category.

One of these smaller, but healthy, competitors is Kava coffee. There is a group of coffee drinkers who love the brew, but cannot tolerate its acidity. Kava said, "We can't attack Maxwell House or Folgers head on, but we *can* carve out a nice share of the coffee market—those people who suffer from hyperacidity." So Kava appeals to one specific group of coffee drinkers, and to that group, Kava is number one.

When it comes to developing products for special uses, that is, selecting niches based on specific products, no one can tell you as much as your organization should already know. The big thing is not to hide your product differentiation. You've got to go public with your product niche. Even the Bible—Matthew, Chapter 5—tells us not to hide our light under a bushel! "Let your light so shine before men, that they may see your good works."

The third area, the penetration of new markets, requires constant monitoring. Be sure to develop strong relations with your operator community. Your operators can alert you to real opportunities to profit from new markets, if you're flexible enough to take rapid advantage of them.

The final area in niche marketing is the selling of price or added value. No one can maintain the lowest prices all the time, but the companies that do best establish an equity for their brand names. That is the way to sell your products at a reasonable profit, because you have built a demand for that product. Moveover, when you do have a special promotion or provide some added value, the consumer appreciates it.

Niche marketing does work, particularly if you develop the advertising to let the world know. It's essential that the niche be exploited, letting people know so that you establish a clear, honest, credible, and memorable positioning in the minds of the target audience. The question becomes: Do you have the courage and foresight to support a new corporate niche and positioning with the right kind and right amount of advertising?

There is always a way to be number one, profitably, and on your own terms.

A Sample Marketing Plan for your Restaurant

PURPOSE

The purpose of this document is to present to Your Restaurant's management XYZ Consulting's marketing recommendations covering the 12-month period January–December 1993. Included are a series of "next steps," which indicate the action to be taken to bring the elements of the plan to fruition. We thank Your Restaurant, Inc., for the opportunity to complete this plan, and for the cooperation of Your Restaurant's management in providing information and support.

BACKGROUND

Sales

1. Your Restaurant is one of the *highest sales volume* restaurants (in the top 1 percent) in the *United States,* at an annual level in excess of *$5.0 million.*

2. *The business is highly seasonal,* with almost 63 percent of sales generated during the January–May period. The remaining seven months have, historically, produced approximately 37 percent of total annual volume. *Peak months* are February and March, while September and October are the *valley months* (at one-third the weekly sales of the peak periods).

3. *Annual sales have slipped from those of the prior year for both calendar year 1991 and the first 11 months of 1992.* Sales for 1991 were down 9 percent and for 1992 down 4 percent through November.

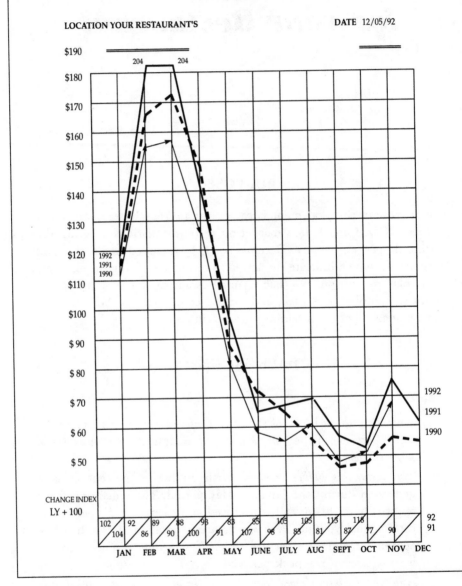

Figure H.1
AVERAGE WEEKLY SALES
($000)

Table H.1
YOUR RESTAURANT'S AVERAGE WEEKLY SALES ($000)

MONTH (WEEKS)		1991	1992	1992 SEASONAL INDEX	1992 CHANGE INDEX	1993	CHANGE INDEX
JANUARY	(5)	120.6	125.2	126	104	127.7	102
FEBRUARY	(4)	204.0	176.2	177	86	162.7	92
MARCH	(4)	204.4	183.9	185	90	163.3	89
APRIL	(5)	155.7	155.2	156	100	136.5	88
MAY	(4)	107.3	97.2	98	91	90.9	93
JUNE	(4)	76.7	81.9	82	107	68.1	83
JULY	(5)	77.5	76.1	77	98	65.0	85
AUGUST	(4)	79.9	66.7	67	83	70.2	105
SEPTEMBER	(4)	68.0	55.4	56	81	58.3	105
OCTOBER	(5)	64.6	55.9	56	87	63.0	113
NOVEMBER	(4)	87.6	67.2	68	77	79.0	118
DECEMBER	(4)	71.7	64.7	65	90		
ANNUAL	(52)	109.4	99.3	100	91	98.5	96 (Thru Nov.)

4. *Monthly sales change (compared to the prior year) has been negative*—for the most part—except for the most recent four months (August–November), when sales exceeded those of a year ago by 5 to 18 points. This apparent turnaround is explained somewhat by very soft sales (down 15 percent) during this period 1992.

(Figure H.1 and Table H.1 detail Your Restaurant's average weekly sales for the period under discussion.)

Meal Period Sales and Traffic

These data differ slightly from the prior data, since they cover a full 12 months (December–November) on a calendar month basis. The prior data viewed 11 months on a weekly structure. The differences are minimal and should not influence conclusions derived from the interpretation of the information.

1. *12 months*—combined *sales* are *off 7 percent,* resulting from an overall *decline* in *customer count* of *8 percent,* while overall *check average* shows a slight *increase* of *2 percent.*
2. From a *sales* perspective, the *weekday dinner* period is the most important, representing *32 percent of total volume.* Dinner on weekends and lunch on weekdays are neck and neck for number two at 22 percent and 21 percent, respectively.
3. *Customer traffic* ranking is quite different, however, where *lunch on weekdays* attracts the greatest numbers at *27 percent of total traffic,* followed by *weekday dinners* (30 percent) and *weekday lunch* (18 percent).

% of Annual Total

Period	Sales	Customers
Dinner W/D	32	20
Dinner W/E	22	14
Lunch W/D	21	27
Lunch W/E	14	18
Breakfast W/D	5	10
Breakfast W/E	6	12

4. Although there are wide swings, quarter to quarter, in both sales and traffic, each meal period's share of business is relatively consis-

tent, except *lunch on weekdays,* which *declines* from peak quarter (first) levels *by 6 share points* during the summer quarter.

| | **Business Quarter** | | | | | |
	Dec– Feb.	Mar.– May	June– Aug.	Sept– Nov.	Range	Diff.
TOTAL SALES %	30	34	18	18	18–34	16
Breakfast W/D	5	5	4	5	4– 5	1
Breakfast W/E	5	6	7	7	5– 7	2
Lunch W/D	24	21	18	20	18–24	6
Lunch W/E	13	14	15	15	13–15	2
Dinner W/D	32	33	32	29	29–33	4
Dinner W/E	20	22	24	23	20–24	4
TOTAL CUSTOMERS	30	34	19	17	17–34	17
Breakfast W/D	11	10	9	9	9–11	1
Breakfast W/E	10	12	13	13	10–13	2
Lunch W/D	30	26	24	25	24–30	6
Lunch W/E	17	17	19	20	17–20	2
Dinner W/D	20	21	20	19	19–21	4
Dinner W/E	12	14	15	14	12–15	4

5. *Dinner on weekdays (Sunday through Thursday)* has experienced the greatest decline, with sales off by over $200,000 and traffic count being down in excess of 10,000 customers.

| | **Dinner (Sunday through Thursday)** | | |
	1990/91	*1991/92*	*Diff.*
Sales	$1,799,800	$1,597,200	($202,600)
Customers	76,900	66,200	(10,700)
Check Avg.	$ 23.40	$ 24.12	+.72

6. *Dinner on weekends (Friday and Saturday)* shows a 5 percent drop in sales, while customer count declined 9 percent.

Dinner (Friday and Saturday)

	1990/91	1991/92	Diff.
Sales	$1,132,600	$1,078,600	($54,000)
Customers	49,600	45,300	(4.3)
Check Avg.	$ 22.83	$ 23.81	+.98

7. The *weekday lunch period* shows a *decline* of roughly *$1,000 per week* resulting from a weekly traffic of 111 customers.

Lunch (Monday through Friday)

	1990/91 ($000)	1991/92 ($000)	Index #	Diff. ($000)
Sales	$1,123.0	$1,069.5	95	($53.5)
Customers	95.4	89.6	94	(5.8)
Check Avg.	$ 11.77	$ 11.94	101	+.18

8. *Weekend lunch* is *down $42,700* on a loss of 3,900 customers.

Lunch (Saturday and Sunday)

	1990/91 ($000)	1991/92 ($000)	Index #	Diff. ($000)
Sales	$754.4	$711.7	94	($42.7)
Customers	62.6	58.7	94	(3.9)
Check Avg.	$ 12.05	$ 12.12	101	+.07

9. The *breakfast meal periods*—which collectively represent 11 percent of sales and 22 percent of customers—experienced *slight sales growth* and *flat customer counts* over the 12-month period.

Sales Trends

During 1992, Your Restaurant's overall business was down and flat for the first three quarters, but has rebounded substantially during the last quarter.

1) *Breakfast weekdays* had a strong first quarter (106), bottomed out during March through May (89), and have improved steadily since.

2) *Breakfast weekends* have narrowed the year-ago variance at an increasing rate each quarter—from a first quarter level of 90 to 120 during the last quarter.

3) *Lunch weekdays* have performed similar to breakfast weekends—90 to 122.

4) Lunch weekends rebounded from a poor first quarter (88) with a 97 during the second quarter, and are at 109 during the latest period.

5) *Dinner weekdays* have trended similar to lunch weekends (93 to 81 to 103).

6) *Dinner weekends* are also similar (98 to 91 to 113).

Change Index (Prior Year-100) by Quarter

MEAL PERIODS	Dec– Feb.	Mar.– May	June– Aug.	Sept– Nov.	Range	Diff.
TOTAL SALES	92	89	90	112	93	
Breakfast W/D	106	91	99	126	102	
Breakfast W/E	90	94	97	120	103	
Lunch W/D	90	93	94	122	95	
Lunch W/E	88	97	89	109	94	
Dinner W/D	93	81	87	103	89	
Dinner W/E	98	91	94	113	95	
TOTAL CUSTOMERS	91	90	89	109	92	
Breakfast W/D	103	93	102	119	102	
Breakfast W/E	99	97	94	120	99	
Lunch W/D	89	92	93	118	94	
Lunch W/E	86	98	92	100	94	
Dinner W/D	89	80	81	98	86	
Dinner W/E	99	88	84	113	91	

Trading Area Definition

Customer zip code data were culled from a total of 493 comment cards (permanent residents) and 179 customer surveys. The data indicate that business is generated from a wide geographic area, characterizing Your Restaurant as a destination facility, particularly during the dinner meal period (weekday and weekend) and weekend breakfast and lunch.

Geographically, the bulk of customers are drawn, or can be motivated to visit, from within these boundaries:

North—Smithtown
West—Washingtonville
East—Mooretown
South—South Chester

Customer Surveys

XYZ Consulting conducted surveys among customers during each of the six meal periods to gain a sampling of their purchase habits and perceptions of Your Restaurant. A total of 176 interviews were completed.

1. Customers *visit* Your Restaurant an average of *1.4 times per month.* Highest frequency meal periods are breakfast and dinner on weekends.

Visit Frequency (per Month)

Period	#	5	2	1	.25	First	Avg.
B - W/D	8	63	13	—	25	—	3.5
B - W/E	47	19	6	23	28	24	1.8
L - W/D	10	10	10	10	60	10	1.1
L - W/E	51	10	6	14	49	22	1.1
D - W/D	18	0	0	17	56	28	0.4
D - W/E	38	11	3	3	42	41	1.8
TOTAL	176	14	6	14	42	24	1.4

2. The *main reason* customers go to Your Restaurant is the *view* of the water.

Main Visit Motivation (%)

View	51%
Recommendation	15%
Nearby	8%
Ads	2%
Other	24%

3. During the survey period (Nov. 91) 64 *percent* of Your Restaurant customers were *year-round* Florida residents, while *21 percent* were *seasonal* residents.

Florida Status

Local Resident	64%
Seasonal Resident	21%
Other	15%

4. Customers travel an *average of 13 miles* to Your Restaurant. They travel 8 miles for breakfast, 16 for lunch, and 12 for dinner.

Distance Traveled (Miles) (%)

Period	#	1	1–5	5–10	10–15	15+	30+	Avg.
B - W/D	8	25	25	25	—	12	13	8
B - W/E	47	9	43	11	13	17	6	8
L - W/D	10	10	30	10	10	0	40	15
L - W/E	51	0	22	12	12	16	39	17
D - W/D	18	11	33	11	0	17	28	13
D - W/E	38	11	24	16	5	26	18	12
TOTAL	176	7	31	13	9	18	23	13

5. *The typical average party size was three people,* with parties of two being most common.

Party Size

Alone	2
Two	43
Three	18
Four	26
Five +	11
Avg.	3

6. *Customers rate Your Restaurant "good to excellent" in very high numbers for food, service, and friendliness.* The prices category received many more "average" ratings than the other attributes. Very few negatives were expressed.

Absolute Ratings (%)

	Exc.	Good	Avg.	Fair	Poor
Food	48	40	10	—	2
Service	50	33	10	3	3
Friendliness	65	28	5	1	1
Prices	22	40	28	9	0

7. When compared with competition, Your Restaurant is considered *better than, or, at least, similar to* competitors for food, service, and friendliness. *Prices* had an overall *lower rating,* with 20 percent indicating a "worse" price rating versus competition.

Relative Ratings (%)

	Much Better	Better	Similar	Worse	Much Worse
Food	15	23	47	15	0
Service	13	29	53	5	0
Friendliness	11	26	57	6	0
Prices	7	13	60	20	0

8. Customers think primarily older couples dine at Your Restaurant.

Who Dines at Your Restaurant (%)

Young Couples	11
Singles	2
Families	9
Older Couples	48
Other	30

9. Females are 57 percent of the customer mix, and the average is 48 years.

Sex	Male	43%
	Female	57%

Age

Range	
18–24	1
25–34	20
35–49	32
50–64	27
65+	20
Avg.	48

Competition

Your Restaurant's competition is countywide and beyond. Your Restaurant is a destination location and draws customers from as far north as Smithtown and as far south as Chester and South Chester. In the broadest definition of the term "competition," *all restaurants* located within these geographic boundaries can be considered competition for Your Restaurant.

The vast majority of Your Restaurant's customers (as indicated in customer surveys and comments to the restaurant staff) choose Your Restaurant when seeking a *waterfront dining experience.* Therefore, for our purposes, Your Restaurant's primary competition has been identified as *waterfront restaurants in Washington County.* Those restaurants specifically identified by Your Restaurant's customers and management as primary competition are Smiling Swordfish, Talbots, and Chumley's. Four Seasons and Westgate Cafe should also be considered competition, but were mentioned less frequently by customers.

Prior to the opening of Chumley's in 1984, Your Restaurant held a unique niche as the only waterfront restaurant in Washington County. Since that time, several other waterfront establishments have opened their doors in close proximity to Your Restaurant, thus eliminating its uniqueness.

Your Restaurant lunch prices are competitive. Your Restaurant dinner prices are generally higher than its competitors. This price distinction is exacerbated by the fact that all competitors, with the exception of Smiling Swordfish, include a salad with entrees. Your Restaurant and Smiling Swordfish feature a la carte menus. *Your Restaurant is the only waterfront restaurant that offers breakfast.* The majority of the other restaurants do, however, offer Sunday brunch.

Waterfront Restaurants

Restaurant	Price Range	Typical Entree
Lunch		
Chumley's	Not Open	N/A
Talbots	$ 3.95–$11.95	$ 5.95–$11.50
Smiling Swordfish	$ 3.50–$11.50	$ 5.50–$11.50
Four Seasons	$ 4.95–$ 7.95	$ 5.95
Westgate	$ 4.95–$ 9.95	$ 6.95
Your Restaurant	$ 3.95–$16.95	$ 5.95–$10.95
Restaurant	*Price Range*	*Typical Entree*
Dinner		
Chumley's	$10.95–$24.95	$16.95
Talbots	$ 8.50–$24.95	$11.95–$14.95
Smiling Swordfish	$14.50–$23.00	$17.00–$19.00
Four Seasons	$ 8.95–$21.95	$15.00
Westgate	$ 9.95–$14.95	$12.95
Your Restaurant	$ 9.95–$27.95	$17.95–$18.95

Menu

Your Restaurant offers distinct menus for each meal period. Your Restaurant is in the process of installing a new menu, which has more breadth in the mid-price range of entrees. The new menu will also include a signature Caesar salad with all entrees.

The old menu offerings are as follows. The *breakfast menu* consists of a variety of unique and unusual breakfast offerings, as well as traditional favorites. Prices range from $1.65 to $7.95. The *lunch menu* features many of the same items offered on the dinner menu, at lower prices, as well as deli sandwiches and burgers. Prices range from $3.95 to $16.95. The *dinner menu* features predominantly seafood items, and offers both traditional and innovative preparations. Prices range from $9.95 to $27.95. Previous management changed the menu to an a la carte menu, without reducing prices. This action prompted numerous customer complaints, and exacerbated the existing price/value problem.

Operations Assessment

Your Restaurant's operations were assessed by XYZ Consulting's team of seasoned restaurant "critics" during November and December 1992, primarily during the dinner period. Following each visit, XYZ Consulting's team completed evaluation forms, describing their experiences at Your Restaurant and rating the food, beverages, service, and overall experience on a scale of 1 (low) to 5 (high). The averaged ratings are as follows:

Service	4.2
Beverage	4.7
Food	4.2
Overall	3.9

Service was inconsistent, with half of the evaluations citing inattentive, slow, or "casual" service, and half praising the service as outstanding. *Beverages were judged very good* by all, with specific comments pertaining to the excellent garnish/presentation. *Food was judged very good,* particularly the presentation. Several comments were made about the lack of attention to "details" of foodservice—specifically, slow correction of items sent back, as well as not being offered fresh pepper or sour cream.

As indicated above, the overall ratings were slightly lower than ratings for the individual components of the dining experience. Comments on the evaluation forms indicate that this discrepancy is due to the *price/value perception.* Although the food, beverages, and service were considered very good, the meal was not considered to be worth the price.

Prior Marketing Activities

Prior marketing activities and advertising materials have focused primarily on Your Restaurant's *image and location,* using mass media (print and television) in the Washington and Lincoln County areas. JKL Marketing has served as Your Restaurant's advertising agency since December 1986.

Highlights and results of prior marketing activities include:

- *Operations problems have destroyed several otherwise successful campaigns.* The introduction of the new menu and the Thanksgiving promotion of 1987 both drew in large crowds, which the operation was unable to handle satisfactorily.

- *Marketing direction from Your Restaurant's previous owners has been erratic and not focused.*
- *The marketing budget has ranged from a low of 3.5 percent of sales to a high of 6 percent. Annual expenditures have ranged from $125,000 to in excess of $375,000.*

Management Comments

During a planning session held in October, Your Restaurant's management staff was asked questions pertaining to the competition, the marketing, and the operation of the restaurant.

Management opinions voiced at this session include:

- *Your Restaurant caters to three different markets:* short-term tourists (two-week maximum stay), seasonal residents (three- to five-month stay), and permanent residents.
- *The casual, "Florida" ambience of the facility does not match the menu, prices, and service style.*
- *Perceived value is a problem,* particularly at dinner.
- *Liquor sales were discouraged by previous management.*
- *The management staff would not choose Your Restaurant for a dining experience* for a variety of reasons (too expensive, older crowd, not as much fun as other restaurants).
- *Previous owners maximized cash flow in the operation* to the detriment of the business.
- *Service is better than, or comparable to all competitors.* Server training, however, could be improved.
- *Marketing opportunities not previously exploited* include banquet/catering facilities, product promotions, and internal promotions/merchandise.

Employee Attitudes

Questionnaires, addressing a variety of issues, were distributed to Your Restaurant's employees, with stamped and addressed envelopes to ensure their confidentiality. Questionnaires were returned by 16 Your Restaurant employees. Highlights of the responses are as follows:

- Primary customer comments concern the wonderful location (50%), high prices (44%), good food (38%), and lack of docking facilities (25%).

- Virtually all feel Your Restaurant is better than or comparable to competition.

- Many employees feel that promotions are explained adequately to the staff, but *only in response to staff questions.*

Barriers to Success

Barriers to success are those factors that inhibit the sales growth potential of Your Restaurant. In Your Restaurant's case, several of these barriers can be overcome with time and effort.

1. *Image*—Your Restaurant's image reportedly has deteriorated during the past few years. A series of ownership changes has left consumers confused, and actions taken by previous owners to maximize profitability damaged the restaurant's reputation. Local residents consider Your Restaurant to be a "tourist trap."

2. *Loss of Unique Niche*—Until a few years ago, Your Restaurant enjoyed a unique niche as one of the few waterfront restaurants in Washington County. The advent of several new waterfront restaurants in Washington County eliminated the uniqueness of Your Restaurant's location.

3. *Lack of Docking Facilities*—Your Restaurant's lack of available docking facilities eliminates the restaurant as a choice among those who wish to visit a waterfront restaurant by boat.

4. *Inconsistent Conceptual Components*—Your Restaurant's ambience, menu, and service style do not convey a consistent positioning to the consumer. The casual decor, staff uniforms, and service style appear to be inconsistent with the menu offerings and price structure ($25 dinner/deck chairs).

How High Is Up at Your Restaurant?

Peak weeks during 1992 served 10,000 customers, generating approximately $170,000. This rate annualizes at over $8.8 million. The business has the capacity to add customers to all meal periods. By increasing weekday traffic count to weekend levels—which is not optimizing—the peak week calculates at 15,500 customers, generating approximately $263,500. This rate annualizes at over $13.7 million.

Increase to weekend levels

Breakfast = Add 400 per day, 5 days = 2,000

Lunch   = Add 400 per day, 5 days = 2,000

Dinner   = Add 300 per day, 5 days = 1,500

Total = 5,500

Weekly Customer Count

Meal Period	Period Peak	Daily Average	Period Average	Daily Average	Period Valley	Daily Average
Breakfast Weekday	1000	200	630	126	400	80
Breakfast Weekend	1200	600	756	378	480	240
Lunch Weekday	2600	520	1638	328	1040	208
Lunch Weekend	1800	900	1134	567	720	360
Dinner Weekday	2000	400	1260	252	800	160
Dinner Weekend	1400	700	882	441	560	280
WEEKLY TOTAL	1000	1429	6300	900	4000	571

Conclusions

1. *Your Restaurant's exalted national sales position should be part of the restaurant's public communication.* The restaurant is one of the highest volume restaurant establishments in Florida, not to mention the country, which is a strong indicator of popularity.

2. Your Restaurant needs a series of *marketing programs* that target its variety of customer segments and are designed to *optimize peak season volumes* and to *generate additional traffic* from among the growing year-round resident population—particularly during the *off-season.* The business appears to be very reliant on seasonal traffic—seasonal residents, visitors, and vacationers—in and out of the greater Charney area, reflected by the dramatic range of absolute sales levels throughout the year. This sales pattern is typical of southwestern Florida restaurants situated along the waterways. However, the population trend in the area, particularly in the Washington/Lincoln County market, is toward a greater number of year-round residents. Over time, this trend should tend to flatten the business's sales graph, primarily by lifting the lower volume sales months.

3. *Recent monthly total sales growth*—August–November 1992—*depicts a turnaround trend,* which needs to be continued throughout 1993. Marketing activities that contribute to this continued growth are needed for the entire year.

4. Customer purchase habits by meal period are fairly consistent throughout the year. *Therefore, no single meal period—or periods—influences total sales to a significant degree.* This may well be the result of advertising programs that have focused on Your Restaurant as a physical destination, without much emphasis on individual meal periods.

5. *Weekend dinner business* presents the biggest meal period sales-building opportunity, manifested by its decline in sales and traffic, and should receive direct marketing attention.

6. *Dinner on weekdays* is the second priority meal period, followed by lunch all week—but marketed by weekpart. Marketing programs are needed to address these three distinct meal period opportunities.

7. *Breakfast,* although low on the priority list—sales are up a bit and, as a percent of business it is only 11 percent—should receive marketing support to improve growth and to attempt to convert the period's high customer count (22 percent of total) into patrons during other meal periods.

8. Customer average *purchase frequency* of 1.4 times per month *could be increased,* particularly with marketing programs that encourage customer movement to other "natural" meal periods, such as breakfast to lunch weekdays or dinner weekdays to breakfast weekends.

9. Your Restaurant's *waterfront view* should be an *important,* but not the only, *part* of the restaurant's consumer communications. Research indicates that 51 percent of respondents said the "view" was the main reason for visiting.

10. Your Restaurant's marketing activities should take into account *the lifestyles of the southwestern Florida populace,* which is made up of year-round residents, seasonal residents, and tourists.

11. Since customers are willing to travel great (relatively) distances—an average of 13 miles—it is concluded the *restaurant is a destination* to most customers. It is suspected impulse purchases are few. Further, the "great distance" data highlight the need for extensive geographical media coverage to reach the likely target market.

12. Your Restaurant's *enormous customer base* should provide the media foundation for the business. A customer mailing list should be created, maintained, and used on a continuous basis.

13. The restaurant's *key attributes* of good friendly service and high quality ratings—in absolute terms—*should form the basis of Your Restaurant's positioning statement.*

14. Your Restaurant's *new menu should be promoted.* A great deal of thought and effort have gone into designing a menu that will communicate a better price/value perception than the current menu. Promotion of the new menu will help dispel the image of Your Restaurant as "too expensive."

15. Your Restaurant has lost market share to the competition. *An aggressive marketing stance should be taken to gain retrial* from customers who now dine elsewhere.

16. Several marketing programs in the past have proven to be *too* successful for the operation to handle. Each promotion's potential impact on business and Your Restaurant's operational *readiness* should be assessed prior to the implementation of any marketing program to avoid this problem in the future.

17. *Steps should be taken to improve Your Restaurant's image in the community.* Marketing programs that incorporate community involvement should be implemented.

18. The restaurant's fuzzy positioning has served to confuse customers in the past. *Your Restaurant must take steps to ensure that the agreed upon positioning of the concept is carried through* (particularly at dinner) in every aspect of the operation, as well as in all marketing efforts.

19. Your Restaurant's location and numerous dining areas create an ideal facility for group functions. In 1992, over $400,000 in banquet sales were generated, with very little marketing effort. *A proactive group business solicitation effort should be implemented.*

20. There exists an *opportunity to generate repeat business from first-time triers,* who represent 24 percent of researched customers.

MARKETING RECOMMENDATIONS

Included in this section is a series of strategic and tactical recommendations for the January–December 1993 period.

Sales Goals

Due to wide swings in growth, the 1993 forecast is based on the average share data for each month over the past two years.

Month	# of Weeks	Weekly Average	Total Sales	C.I.
JANUARY	5	$124.8	$ 624.0	98
FEBRUARY	4	190.4	761.6	117
MARCH	4	192.6	770.4	118
APRIL	5	154.5	772.5	113
MAY	4	103.7	414.8	114
JUNE	4	80.4	321.6	118
JULY	5	78.3	391.5	120
AUGUST	4	74.1	296.4	106
SEPTEMBER	4	62.4	249.6	107
OCTOBER	5	60.3	301.5	96
NOVEMBER	4	78.3	313.2	99
DECEMBER	4	69.8	279.2	103
TOTAL	52	105.7	$5496.3	107
BANQUET SALES			$1200.0	

These gains are anticipated to be due to increased customer count, while maintaining the current check average. The primary focus of the marketing programs presented in this document is targeted toward this objective.

Marketing Strategies

Your Restaurant will attempt to achieve these marketing goals by:

1. Attracting sufficient *customer traffic* from among each *target market* for each *meal period* during each of the *two major seasons.*
2. Encouraging increased *customer visit frequency* from among the *established customer base,* current *infrequent users,* and *new triers* at Your Restaurant.
3. *Generating groups and party business* to maximize use of the areas available that accommodate sizable parties.

Programs designed to focus sales-building activities in support of each strategy have been developed. The building of check average will play a secondary role to the strategies indicated above, due to the apparent existing price/value problem.

Communications Strategy

While each piece of advertising generally requires its own advertising strategy/focus, it is important for Your Restaurant to adopt and embrace umbrella strategies in the form of a *positioning statement* and a *brand personality* to form the basis of its consumer communications.

The following attributes were assessed in absolute terms, and then relative to the competition, based on customer surveys as well as XYZ Consulting's opinions.

Attribute	Absolute	Relative to Competition
Good food	Good	Equal
Attentive, friendly service	Good	Equal
Variety	Fair	Worse
Good value	Fair	Worse
Ambience	Good	Better
Entertaining	Poor	Worse
Cleanliness	Fair	Equal
Comfort	Fair	Worse
Recognition	Good	Better

Positioning

Your Restaurant provides the best dining experience in an open-air, waterfront setting in Washington County. The restaurant is extremely popular, as manifested by its position as one of the highest volume restaurants in the state of Florida. The excellent food and friendly, attentive service are perfect complements to the scenic view and Florida ambience.

Personality

Your Restaurant is the Florida you've always dreamed about. Lush tropical walkways; soft, gentle breezes; majestic yachts gliding by as you feast on a perfectly prepared and presented meal. You feel pampered by the friendly, attentive, polished staff who cater to your every wish, while you relax and enjoy the beautiful view and comfortable ambience. You feel welcome as you enter your dream, just as seafarers felt welcomed by the comforting sound of the waves gently caressing the shoreline. This is the Florida you've always dreamed about—and have finally found.

Media Strategies

Each marketing program requires media vehicles to deliver the sales message to Your Restaurant's target market for each dining occasion.

Here are the recommended media approaches to reach and influence the various consumer segments:

1. *Dinner—All Days*

Who	Family income = $35,000 +
	Age = 25 yrs. +
	Residents
	Retirees
	Vacationers
	Visitors to area
Where	Washington County
	Lincoln County
	During season = 40 minutes travel
	Off season = 20 minutes travel
Desires	Good food
	Waterfront location
	Relaxed atmosphere
	Unrushed dining time
Media	Washington County print
	Lincoln County print
	Direct mail to residents
	Television
	Radio
	Your Restaurant's customer list
	In-restaurant communications
	Hotel publications and distribution
	Entertainment publications

2. *Breakfast and Lunch—Weekdays*
    Who   White-collar businesspeople
                  Residents
                  Visitors
                  Vacationers
                  Retirees

    Where   Washington County
                  Lincoln County
                  Within 15 minutes travel time

    Desires   Good food
                  Beautiful location
                  Reasonable prices
                  Fast service
                  Easy access

    Media   Your Restaurant's customer list
                  Washington County print
                  Lincoln County print
                  Television
                  Radio
                  In-restaurant communications
                  Direct mail to businesses
                  Direct sales to businesses
                  Hotel publications and distribution
                  Telemarketing to businesses

3. *Breakfast and Lunch—Weekends*
    Who   Family income = $35,000 +
                  Age = 25 yrs. +
                  Residents
                  Retirees
                  Vacationers
                  Visitors

    Where   Washington County
                  Lincoln County
                  Within 40 minutes travel time

    Desires   Good food
                  Waterfront location
                  Relaxed atmosphere
                  Unrushed dining time

Media	Washington County print
	Lincoln County print
	Television
	Radio
	Your Restaurant's customer list
	In-restaurant communications
	Hotel publications and distribution

4. *Group Business—Selected Meal Periods*

Who	Organizations
	Businesses
	Private parties
Where	Washington County
	South Chester to Smithtown
Desires	Waterfront location
	Good food
	Isolated meeting area
	Dedicated service
	Special group prices
Media	Direct mail
	Direct sales
	In-restaurant communications

Note: An important component of the plan is the use of the Your Restaurant's customer list as a media vehicle. Your Restaurant is encouraged to expand its list and to maintain it in-house or with an outside supplier. The cost to input data is $250 per thousand. Running labels is a minimal expense at 2¢ each.

Budget Strategy

From a planning perspective, it is recommended that Your Restaurant budget marketing spending at 5 percent of planned sales to cover production and media expenses. This 5 percent level would result in an annual budget of $335,300. (This level may require adjustment once the marketing plan is fully developed and priced.)

Month	Sales	Budget
JANUARY	$ 624.0	$ 32.9
FEBRUARY	761.6	38.1
MARCH	770.4	38.5

Month	Sales	Budget
APRIL	772.5	38.6
MAY	414.8	20.7
JUNE	321.6	16.1
JULY	391.5	20.0
AUGUST	296.4	14.8
SEPTEMBER	249.6	12.5
OCTOBER	301.5	15.1
NOVEMBER	313.2	15.7
DECEMBER	279.2	14.0
RESTAURANT TOTAL	5496.3	275.3
BANQUET TOTAL	1200.0	60.0
TOTAL	$6696.3	$335.3

Scheduling Strategy

Here is the recommended scheduling of marketing and media activities for calendar 1993.

1. *Your Restaurant's Customers (mailing list)*
   A. Collect customer names and addresses year-round.
   B. Ensure Florida residency status—year-round resident, seasonal resident, and/or annual visitor—is indicated on each file.
   C. Ensure data is merged to avoid duplicate mailings.
   D. Mail to *year-round residents* each quarter of the year with an appropriate visit incentive.
   E. Mail to *seasonal residents* a "We're looking forward to seeing you" message in a Christmas card (December), and mail once again toward the season's end with a visit incentive (March).
   F. Mail to *annual visitors* once using the Christmas card device.
2. *Vacationers/Visitors/Residents*
   A. Advertise each week in the entertainment section of the selected media—quarter-page, fixed position. This is where visitors look for dining and entertainment information.
   B. During the season, advertise Your Restaurant's offering—no promotion needed.
   C. After Easter, advertise incentive promotion offers to stimulate traffic among year-round residents and area visitors.
   D. Advertise in hotel publications (in-room) year round.

E. Arrange distribution of Your Restaurant's promotion piece via targeted hotels' concierge desks.

3. *Residents*
   A. Conduct targeted direct marketing promotions to selected names (lists) four times per year to expand customer base.
   B. Geographic targets: Washington and Lincoln Counties.
   C. Distribution could be via bulk delivery (condos), direct mail, and/or freestanding inserts.

4. *Your Restaurant's Customers* (in-restaurant)
   A. Use table cards and chalk board announcements of other meal periods and special promotion events.
   B. Install a staff sales incentive contest to build per customer expenditure. Incentive contests will be conducted every other month.

5. *Business from Businesses*
   A. Conduct four (quarterly) drive periods against trading area businesses to build breakfast and lunch traffic.
   B. Direct sales, direct mail, telemarketing, and other programs should be employed during drive periods.

6. *Group Business*
   A. Conduct four (quarterly) drive periods in an effort to schedule year-round groups at Your Restaurant.
   B. Include party suggestions in all direct solicitation programs to customers and residents.

Promotion Strategy

Since Your Restaurant's marketing history indicates very little in the way of promotion activity, promotion incentives will be employed on a *selective* basis against specific markets in order to maintain Your Restaurant's concept integrity.

1. There will be occasions when *"rich" incentives* will be called for, particularly when *"trial" among new potential customers* or *"retrial" from former customers* is the goal. Such "rich" offers might take the form of buy one, get one free, a $5.00 dining certificate, or a free bottle of wine.

2. Promotion incentives that encourage and reward *purchase frequency* over specified time periods may be employed.

3. *Modest incentives* used primarily for current customers and during peak or near-peak sales periods might be employed, such complete meal deals for a special price, free dessert, dinner/lunch for two at a special price, or higher priced menu items at a reduced price (item trial).

4. A staff sales incentive contest may be used to encourage higher checks and to *reward staff performance* for helping to generate extra revenue.

5. Discounts, or special packages, should be offered to encourage *group business.*

6. Advertising and in-restaurant activities should take advantage of holidays by:

   Decorating the restaurant in the holiday's theme

   Dressing customer contact staff in the holiday's attire

   Advertising a "Holiday Special" to generate traffic—on holidays that are not already "maxed out"

   Extending the life of the event beyond its one-day life, per the following schedule (# of weeks in brackets):

   - President's Day (1)
   - Valentine's Day (1)
   - St. Patrick's Day (1)
   - Easter (1)
   - Mother's Day (1)
   - Memorial Day (1)
   - Father's Day (1)
   - July Fourth (1)
   - Labor Day (1)
   - Halloween (1)
   - Thanksgiving (1)
   - Christmas (3)
   - New Year's (1)
   - Secretary's Day (1)

Your Restaurant should run special *consumer promotions* throughout the year to boost sales (see Figure H.3). *Four major consumer promotions* will be planned for 1993. *Preplanning and arranging* for each event should start at least *four weeks prior* to the actual kickoff.

Figure H.3
YOUR RESTAURANT'S MARKETING ACTIVITIES CALENDAR

199___	JAN.	FEB.	MAR.	APR.	MAY	JUNE	JULY	AUG.	SEPT.	OCT.	NOV.	DEC.
CONSUMER ADVERTISING												
Holidays	X	XX	X	XX	XX	X	X	X	X	X	X	XX
3rd Anniversary	|-----	-----|				|-----	-----|					
New Early Bird Menu												
Food Festivals									|-----	-----|		
Special Menu Items												
Discount Coupons	X	X	X	X	X	X		X	X	X	X	X
CUSTOMER MARKETING												
- Year Round			X	X								
- Seasonal											X	X
- Annual												X
RESEARCH												
CAP Study		|-----|						|---|				
IN-STORE PROMOTIONS												
- Birthday Club	Start											
- Drive Thrus	Set - Up	Use as	Needed --									
- Crew Incentives	A	B	A	B	A	B	A	B	A	B	A	B
- VIP Program	Set - Up	Start										
- Sunday Brunch	Set - Up	Start										
- Bouncebacks		test -----			|-- test --							
- Frequency Cards							|-----	-----|				
- Gift Certificates		Set - Up										
DIRECT MARKETING												
- Fundraisers	Set - Up											
- Groups/Parties	Set - Up	X	X	X	X	X	X	X	X	X	X	X
- Chef's Table				X	X	X	X	X	X	X	X	X
- Hotel Guests	Start			X			X			X		
- Weddings	Set - Up			X	X	X	X				X	
- Gold Coast	Confirm			Start	Test -----							-Finish
- Gourmet Service					Test -----							-Finish

Each event will be *promoted and advertised* to maximize awareness and generate traffic. *Media* may include direct mail, newspapers, inserts, radio, and television. *In-house merchandising* should also be used, including table tents and special employee buttons. *Employee involvement* will be an important element in each event. The staff should be well informed of the promotion details and timing. Also, a *suggestive selling program* or other employee contests should be included with each event.

Each promotion will involve a specific *theme,* and will focus on specific *menu items.*

The following are guidelines for recommended themes:

- New Menu Introduction—The new menu is designed to change the perception of the price/value at Your Restaurant. An advertising campaign highlighting the new menu will communicate this to the consumers.

- A New Look at Your Restaurant—An advertising campaign to create some excitement about the newly renovated Your Restaurant.

- "Anniversary Celebration"—An anniversary promotion, celebrating Your Restaurant's 15th season as one of Florida's most popular restaurants. Consumer incentives should be involved.

- Selected Product Promotions—Promotion involving Your Restaurant's signature items. Consumer incentives should be involved.

DECK DOINGS

Target Market: Permanent residents, seasonal residents, and tourists from Washington and Lincoln Counties.

Description: Deck Doings are all-day events held once a month. They may be planned to coincide with holidays, community events, fishing tournaments, or other special activities. Offer free hors d'oeuvres, special beverage prices, and/or giveaway items as incentives. Whenever possible, tie in with local radio stations. Vendor support should be used. Preliminary suggested themes are:

Your Restaurant Limbo

- Calypso/Reggae band waterside
- Limbo contest
- Liquor vendor support promos

Margaritaville in May
- Specially priced Margaritas
- Jimmy Buffet-style entertainment
- "Hamburger in Paradise"—hamburger with out-of-the-ordinary side order, like fried shrimp or scallops, for a special price.

Materials: Fliers
Posters in restrooms

Timing: Monthly

DIRECT CONSUMER MARKETING

Target Market: Residents of, and visitors to, Washington and Lincoln Counties.

Description: Your Restaurant should conduct a series of direct marketing programs during the course of the year targeting high potential residents (via direct mail) and/or likely potential geographic areas (via newspaper inserts). Direct marketing programs demand the use and application of consumer incentives, which will be developed. A suggested device to employ for either direct marketing approach is a Your Restaurant customer newspaper (separate discussion).

Materials: Customer newspaper
Other direct marketing devices

Timing: One event per quarter—January, April, July, and October

YOUR RESTAURANT CUSTOMER MAILINGS

Target Market: Your Restaurant's customers

Description: Your Restaurant should collect names, addresses, and residency status of all customers who choose to be informed of Your Restaurant's activities via the mails. The mailing list should sort customers by residency status as well as geography. Out-of-Florida addresses should be collected for non year-round residents, as well as their Florida address. Promotional mailings to each segment of the list should be conducted using the customer newspaper and other direct mail techniques.

Materials: Customer registration forms
Customer newspaper
Christmas card
Other direct mail devices

Timing: Year-round residents—once per quarter
Seasonal residents—December and March
Annual visitors—December

BIRTHDAY CLUB

Target Market: Your Restaurant's customers—the week of their birthday and possibly other times.

Description: Your Restaurant should help customers celebrate their birthday and thank them for their patronage with a free dinner. No purchase is required. A Your Restaurant "happy birthday" card is mailed to the "birthday customer" a couple weeks prior to the birthday. The card is presented the week of the birthday. Seasonal residents can bring the card in during the season to celebrate their "Florida birthday."

Materials: Sign-up forms
Birthday cards/envelopes

Timing: Start collecting registrants during January; it's a continuous program. Commence mailings as soon as possible.

BUSINESSES OF THE WEEK—The Your Restaurant "Hit" List

Target Market: Businesses of 10 or more employees located within 15 minutes of Your Restaurant.

Description: Each Monday, the Your Restaurant's representative telephones selected businesses to announce, "This is Your Company Week at Your Restaurant. And, to salute you, and thank you for your business, we are pleased to offer a 15 percent discount to your employees, who come in for lunch, or a free cocktail to those who come in for dinner. All the employees have to do is present a business card or letterhead of your company/firm. Please tell everyone." Upon arrival at Your Restaurant, the entrance board will say: "Your Restaurant Salutes Businesses of the Week" WELCOME! This promotion can be a useful vehicle for generating business at the new outside bar and trial of the grazing menu. Select three to five businesses each week. When all area businesses are covered, start over. Make certain service staff is aware of this promotion and make a bit of a fuss over the respondents.

Materials: Entrance board

Timing: Each week of the year when lunch and/or dinner needs extra help.

SERVER INCENTIVE PROGRAM

Target Market: Your Restaurant's current customers

Description: Periodic incentive programs, when coupled with suggestive sales training, will turn Your Restaurant's service staff into a team of eager salespeople. Two recommended approaches are:

1. *Average Check Contest.* Each meal period, the server with the highest check average receives a $25 bonus. The use of this approach ensures that *all* servers attempt to boost their sales throughout the shift. The average check for each server is calculated at the end of the shift, and the incentive awarded in cash that day.

2. *Sales Points.* Each meal period, *each* server who achieves an average per guest expenditure higher

than a preset limit receives points toward prizes. For example, if the preset limit for lunch is $11.50, each server with a higher check average than $11.50 would receive points. The points can be redeemed at the end of the program for Your Restaurant merchandise, gift certificates, or merchandise (i.e., CD players) obtained through tradeouts with other retailers.

Materials: Staff memo

Timing: Implement one of the two programs every other month.

VIP PROGRAM

Target Market: Your Restaurant's current frequent customers

Description: During the peak season, Your Restaurant's loyal customers (permanent and seasonal residents) have difficulty enjoying their favorite restaurant due to the large crowds, long waits, and policy of no reservations. This problem can be turned into an opportunity by recognizing loyal customers through a VIP program. Customers become a VIP *by management invitation only.* Parameters should be set for eligibility (i.e., dines at least once a week, dines once a month but with a large group, etc.), but the final decision is, of course, up to management discretion. When customers are invited to join the program, the manager obtains their name, address(es), birthdates for customer and spouse, and anniversary date. This information is added to Your Restaurant's customer mailing list.

Membership in the VIP Program entitles customers to:

- A *special card,* identifying them as a VIP. It includes the telephone number of a private VIP line. A special VIP pin may also be given to these customers, so they can be readily identified at the door.

- *Reservations or priority seating.* Management may elect to either permit VIPs to make reservations or to seat them ahead of others on the waiting list.
- *Quarterly cocktail parties.* These parties can be used as a forum to solicit VIP opinions on new menu items and other contemplated changes.
- *Birthday and anniversary treats.* Special amenities are offered on VIPs' birthdays or wedding anniversaries.

Materials:	Registration cards VIP cards VIP pins
Timing:	Begin in February and continue throughout year.

SUNDAY BRUNCH MENU

Target Market:	Current Sunday breakfast and lunch customers.
Description:	Sunday breakfast and lunch are two of Your Restaurant's strongest business segments. The typically higher average check at Sunday brunch, however, represents an opportunity to increase per person expenditure during this high traffic period. XYZ Consulting recommends that Your Restaurant develop a special brunch menu, to be offered from 10:00 A.M. to 2:30 P.M., in addition to the existing breakfast and lunch menus. Featured items should include a variety of offerings in a higher price range, encouraging tradeups from the regular menus. This promotion can be tested through the use of table tents promoting higher priced specials.
Materials:	Table tents Menus
Timing:	Start in February

BOUNCEBACKS

Target Market:	Current Your Restaurant customers and guests at group events.

Description: Bounceback certificates can be an effective means of building business, when used to accomplish specific objectives. Recommended uses of bouncebacks for Your Restaurant include:

1. *Targeted Meal Periods.* Take advantage of the large customer base at breakfast (22 percent of total customer count) and offer breakfast guests an incentive to visit Your Restaurant during lunch or dinner.

2. *Group Business.* Offer all guests of group business functions an incentive to dine at Your Restaurant on another occasion.

3. *Long Waits.* Offer those guests who leave when informed of a long wait for a table an incentive to return at another time.

Materials: Bounceback certificates

Timing: Test in February and March.

FREQUENT DINING = $10 GIFT

Target Market: Current Your Restaurant customers

Description: Dinner customers receive a "Frequent Fisher" club card following a visit to Your Restaurant. The card has four whale punch marks, which are canceled during each subsequent visit to Your Restaurant over the next two months. When four whales are canceled, the card holder is given a $10 Your Restaurant gift certificate. The first whale is canceled when delivered; the "valid until" date is recorded for two months hence; the gift certificate is good for three months.

Materials: "Frequent Fisher" club cards (classy)
$10 gift certificates
Announcement flier

Timing: Test for three months from May to July and continue if successful.

GIFT TO A FRIEND

Target Market: Friends of current customers.

Description: This promotion offers a unique sales-building opportunity within the framework of a friendly third-
party endorsement. Your Restaurant has built a large
customer base through referrals/recommendations.
Make it easy for satisfied customers to recommend
the restaurant by providing each customer with a
post card with a colorful graphic on one side, using
one of the many appealing photographs already in
use. On the reverse side of the card is space for the
addressee's data, a stamp, the gift giver's name and
address, the gift giver's message, and the details of
the gift. If the card is filled out at the restaurant,
Your Restaurant stamps and mails. If it is filled out
elsewhere, the sender stamps and mails.

Materials: Post card
Stamps

Timing: Test during March–April.
Continue if extra sales/profits are generated.

CANCELED PROMOTIONS

Target Market: Canceled groups/organizations/clubs in Washington
County

Description: Business is generated from the marketing efforts of
canceled groups/organizations/clubs in the Wash-
ington and Lincoln County area. Several approaches
can be used to take advantage of these efforts.

A. *Certificate Sales.* The fundraiser sells Your Restaurant's gift certificates to group members, family,
friends, and the general public, and keeps a predetermined portion (e.g., 25%) of the sales revenue. These certificates are used by the purchasers
to dine at Your Restaurant.

B. *Celebrity Server Night.* A celebrity (local official,
sports team coach, band leader, etc.) serves as a

server or bartender for a designated period on a specific evening. The celebrity distributes fliers announcing the event; a predetermined portion of the revenues generated during that evening are donated to the canceled group.

Opportunities: Professional canceled organizations
School/college classes, clubs, teams
Fraternal groups
Athletic teams (martial arts)
Social clubs
Political groups
Charities
Benevolent organizations
Places of worship
Employee clubs
Hospitals
Theater groups
Senior citizen groups
Youth groups

Materials: Publication advertisement slick
Handout flier (increase size and use as a poster also)

Timing: Based on individual fundraiser's schedule.

GROUPS AND PARTY BUSINESS

Target Market: Groups, organizations, businesses, and private parties in Washington County and within easy reach of Your Restaurant (South Chester to Smithtown).

Description: Your Restaurant should actively pursue this business opportunity with the objective of attracting groups during soft sales periods and, particularly, during the off-season. A detailed banquet/catering program is included under separate cover. Recommended approaches include:

1. *Four-Color Sales Piece.* A four-color sales piece should be developed, visually depicting the terrific view, the food, and private meeting rooms. The four-color piece will be distributed via direct

mail, as a newspaper insert, and used in sales calls
on local businesses. A custom newspaper could be
used as the group business sales piece.

2. *Business after Hours Party.* Host a cocktail party on
the deck, offering complimentary hors d'oeuvres
and cocktails. Area businesspeople are invited to
the party via an invitation in the mail. The party
will demonstrate, firsthand, Your Restaurant's
unique banquet/party capabilities. In addition,
copies of the banquet brochure detailed above can
be distributed.

3. *Hosted Party.* Groups are invited to Your Restaurant for a party by a "partner" with a client list of
potential customers. Your Restaurant provides
the refreshments and has the opportunity to
distribute copies of the sales piece detailed above.
The partner provides a door prize (Your Restaurant can collect names for their mailing list from
the business cards entered), invites the guests,
and has the opportunity to give their personal
sales pitch (subtly).

Materials: Four-color sales piece/custom newspaper
Direct mail letter/invitation

Timing: Hosted parties—each month
Business after hours parties—each month
Sales piece—produced by March 1993

CHEF'S TABLE

Target Market: Executives of local businesses, groups, and organizations in Washington County and within easy reach of
Your Restaurant (South Chester to Smithtown).

Description: Each month invite selected executives (and guests) to
dine with Chef Wade at a special "Chef's Table."
Ideally, the Chef's Table should be located in Your
Restaurant's kitchen (out of the line of action, of
course). Provide the invited guests with their own

copy of the menu from the meal to take home, and after the event, send them a framed picture of them dining with the chef. The Chef's Table provides an opportunity to showcase Your Restaurant's excellent food and service, helps build loyalty to the restaurant among those invited, and provides a good vehicle for soliciting group business. In addition, the Chef's Table provides an opportunity to gain publicity through the media.

Materials: Invitations
Special menu shells
Picture frames

Timing: Once per month, beginning in April

HOTEL GUEST MARKETING

Target Market: Guests at targeted hotels in northern Washington County.

Description: Your Restaurant should expose its concept to area visitors by advertising (nonpromotional) in in-room publications—and by distributing its customer newspaper or promotion piece via the activities desk at the hotels. Your Restaurant's management should personally visit each concierge, inviting each to a gratis dinner at Your Restaurant and requesting distribution of Your Restaurant's promotion piece (s) to inquiring guests. In addition, special parties should be held three or four times per year for key hotel staff members (concierges, bell captain, convention series directors, etc.) and limousine drivers. The parties will demonstrate the Your Restaurant's experience to them, build a sense of loyalty, and remind them to refer their customers to Your Restaurant.

Materials: Customer newspaper

Timing: Advertise each issue (small space)
Contact concierges during January
Restock customer newspapers as needed

WEDDING BUSINESS

Target Market:	Wedding parties in Washington and Lincoln Counties.
Description:	Your Restaurant should host quarterly "bridal shows" with the objective of attracting rehearsal dinner and wedding reception business. Local bridal shops, tuxedo rental stores, florists, and jewelers are invited to display their wares on a selected date at Your Restaurant. Future brides and their families are invited to the party (list is developed from engagement announcements in the paper, as well as lists provided by retail participants). Your Restaurant provides refreshments, and prominently displays table setups, suggested menus, and pictures of previous wedding events held at the restaurant. Retail participants provide prizes to be awarded through a drawing. Addresses obtained through drawing registrations will provide the basis for future mailings (i.e., anniversary and birthday promotions).
Materials:	Letters of invitation
	Registration cards
Timing:	Quarterly

GOLD COAST DINERS CLUB

Target Market:	Members of the Dining Club
Description:	Southwest Florida Coast Diners Club offers a membership for $45, which entitles its members to a complimentary meal when a second meal of equal or greater value is purchased. The card is valid only during the off-season (April–December). There are currently 6,000 members. There is no cost for the participating restaurant except for the free meals. Southwest Florida Coast will provide Your Restaurant with a list of those members who dine at Your Restaurant, which can be added to the Your Restaurant's customer list for later solicitations.
Materials:	All materials are provided by Southwest Florida Coast.

Timing: Must confirm participation with Southwest Florida Coast by January 1. Program begins April, expires in December.

Note: The number of participating restaurants is limited. There is a chance that availability may be closed out.

CHEF WADE'S GOURMET SERVICE

Target Market: Residents of, and visitors to, Washington and Lincoln Counties.

Description: *Chef Wade's Gourmet Service* is a new concept that offers an extra attraction to potential guests. *Your Restaurant has one of the finest chefs in the Washington County area.* Additionally, the other elements of the purchase mix are competitive, at the very least: the location is terrific; service is excellent; the restaurant is comfortable and attractive.

While Your Restaurant has a competitive edge with its food quality, the gourmet service will provide another advantage. The gourmet service is designed to respond directly to the needs of the market by giving it exactly, and literally, what it wants. The concept is simply designed. The customer places the dinner order for a party at least one day in advance. "Your Restaurant will fix any meal of your choice, the way you like it. Just call your order one day in advance, and when you arrive, we'll already have your meal in preparation." Operationally, the chef will need to set up to handle virtually any meal. The order taker needs to be familiar with cooking operations to enable dealing with very unusual orders. A call to the customer to confirm the order will be required the day of the guests' visit.

Materials: Custom newspaper
                    POS materials

Timing: Test over a three-month period (May–July)

Index